You're Invited!
QUILTS AND HOMES TO INSPIRE

By Barb Adams & Alma Allen of Blackbird Designs

You're Invited
Quilts and Homes to Inspire
By Barb Adams & Alma Allen of Blackbird Designs

Editor: Kent Richards
Technical Editor: Jane Miller
Book Design: Amy Robertson
Photography: Aaron T. Leimkuehler
Illustration: Eric Sears, Gary Embrey, Lon Eric Craven,
Alissa Christianson
Production assistance: Jo Ann Groves

Published by:
Kansas City Star Books
1729 Grand Blvd.
Kansas City, Missouri, USA 64108

First edition, first printing
978-1-933466-30-9
Library of Congress Control Number: 2007937714

Printed in the United States of America
by Walsworth Publishing Co., Marceline, MO

To order copies, call StarInfo at (816) 234-4636
and say "Books."

KANSAS CITY STAR
QUILTS
Continuing the Tradition

www.PickleDish.com

Contents

Introduction

Barb and I are always in pursuit of fun and creative "extras" to include along with patterns in our quilt books for *The Kansas City Star*. Since these books are in full color, we can't resist adding more to inspire your creativity. The "extras" in this book are the home tours. You are invited to the homes of three friends who have transformed their living quarters into places that celebrate art, collections and creative endeavors.

The walls in Joy Hayward's home are filled with her cross-stitch samplers, reminiscent of the needlework taught to young girls in early American schools. As Joy stitches these small works of art, she adds details that commemorate her family's history. A special birthday or anniversary is fondly recalled by Joy as she stitches personal messages onto each sampler.

Sara Larson's home is filled with paintings by her son, Tyler. The colors and subjects of his artwork add a warmth and visual interest to her home. Sara is a multi-talented artist in her own right. Her carved stone cottages and stone sculptures lay hidden amongst flowers in her garden, there to surprise the child in us all. The patience and hard physical labor needed to carve these works of stone are a joy to Sara. "Working on these projects is a great stress reducer," she laughingly relates. Sara loves to recycle old wool sweaters. Her floral chair covers create another life for cast-off sweaters and her pattern is included in this book for you to use.

Maggie Bonanomi's love of nature and simpler times is reflected throughout her home. She takes bits and pieces of this and that and turns them into something wonderful. Vintage textiles and antique pieces are cherished and used for every day. Her artwork reflects this love.

Several designers, new to Blackbird Designs, invite you to try their quilt patterns included in this book along with our designs: Lorraine Hofmann in Little Rock, Arkansas; Yelena Elliott who owns Beechworth Quilters Cottage in Australia; Debbie Roberts who owns The Quilted Moose in Gretna, Nebraska and Sara Larson from Overland Park, Kansas. These designers added whimsical and stylish projects to grace your home.

Barb and I extend an invitation to you to make some quilts, and along the way, experience the wealth of ideas these women share. As you cross these thresholds, we hope you are inspired by creative ideas that stimulate new ways of thinking about home and art. You're invited to explore this book, come with us and share the creativity and style of these women.

Barb and I hope you enjoy your visit!

—*Alma Allen*

ABOVE: A view of the "nature room" in Maggie Bonanomi's home. Among the many things Maggie collects, natural items, like birds' nests, occupy this wonderfully peaceful room. On the wall hangs an antique wool quilt, and draped over the table is "Summer Flags Flying."

Acknowledgments

This book would not have been possible without the contributions of many. Barb and I owe much to the following people: Maggie Bonanomi, Joy Hayward, and Sara Larson all opened their homes for a day of photography. Each was gracious and welcoming as we invaded their homes with photographic equipment.

From our favorite continent down under, Yelena Elliott contributed a quilt celebrating her beloved grandmother. We asked her to share one of her designs with us after seeing her patterns in her quilt shop. We know you will love the soft, scrappy, color palette she has selected for her quilt.

Lorraine Hofmann's meticulous appliquéd quilt is a welcome addition. The internet has expanded the idea of community and enabled us to meet Lorraine and to view her work. We welcome her contribution and know the abundance of bloom in her quilt will add beauty to your home.

A breath of fresh air was added by the updated look of Debbie Roberts' quilt. When we saw what she did with an older pattern of ours, we immediately knew we had to add this one to the book.

Quilts would never be the same without the added texture and design of the quilting stitch. Jeanne Zyck's quilting designs always reflect and enhance our patterns.

Many hours of time must be devoted to bringing projects to completion. The sewing skills of Leona Adams are essential to this endeavor.

Many thanks to my husband, David Allen, who takes the time to read over the text and does the first edit. His technical writing skills are much better than mine, and two heads are always better than one.

Thank you for your continued support and kindness. We hope our friends' creative ideas, the pictures captured in this book, and the quilt patterns and projects will bring you inspiration and hours of pleasure.

Our photographer, Aaron Leimkuehler, has captured the beauty of our friends' homes and quilts through the eye of his camera. It's always a pleasure to work on a project with Aaron.

The talents of Eric Sears of Gary Embrey Design and Lon Eric Craven are essential to this project. Their skills in illustrating the diagrams and patterns bring clarity to the instructions.

Alissa Christianson did the graph for our cross-stitch chart. There is a real artistry to using the symbols to shade the design and make it easy to count and stitch.

The beautiful book design by Amy Robertson binds our efforts into a compelling format. Her vision for the book illuminates our theme.

Photographs must be color corrected for printing, and Jo Ann Groves works in a very small, dark office accomplishing this feat. Any loose threads or problems are digitally corrected by her skills.

No one wants mistakes in their quilting books. Jane Miller shares her mathematical ability as she goes over each and every pattern to make sure there is enough fabric, the correct number of pieces are cut and we are consistent and accurate with our instructions. Believe me, everyone thanks you, Jane!

Many thanks go to our editor, Kent Richards. Kent brings clear, concise instructions through his editing skills.

Finally, thanks belong to you for your continued support and kindness. We hope our friends' creative ideas, the pictures captured by Aaron Leimkuehler, quilt patterns and projects will bring you inspiration and hours of pleasure.

—Alma Allen

RIGHT: Sara Larson's backyard is a such an inviting place. Even outdoors, Sara uses a vintage quilt as a table cover. The pattern of that quilt, Seven Sisters, has always been one of her favorites.

Hand Appliqué Instructions

❖ Make templates of the appliqué shapes using freezer paper or plastic template material. Do not add any seam allowance to these shapes.

❖ If using plastic, trace around the templates on the right side of your fabric. Use a marking pencil that will show up on your fabric. This drawn line indicates your seam line. To cut reversed pieces, flip the plastic template over and trace the reversed shape to the right side of the fabric. If using freezer paper, trace the shapes onto the dull side of the paper. For a reversed piece, trace on the shiny side of the paper. Iron the paper templates, shiny side down, onto the right side of the fabric. Trace around the template. Peel the paper template away carefully, as it can be reused.

❖ After the seam line has been drawn on the right side of the fabric, cut out the shapes, adding a 1/8" − 1/4" seam allowance.

❖ Fold the background fabric in half vertically and horizontally. Finger-press the folds. Open the fabric.

❖ To help achieve placement of the design, refer to the block diagram located with the templates. A one-inch grid is placed over each diagram to indicate position for the pieces. The pieces on our quilts are placed in a whimsical fashion.

❖ Center the design on the background block using the fold lines and placement diagram for assistance.

❖ Baste the shapes into place on the background block with glue stick or appliqué pins. Larger shapes require basting stitches to hold the shapes in place securely.

❖ Use thread that matches your appliqué piece, not the background. Use a two-ply cotton thread that is 50 or 60 weight.

❖ Cut the thread about 12–15" long. Longer threads may become worn and break as you stitch.

❖ For concave curves (curves that go in) clip to the seam line, then turn under the seam allowance. This will allow the fabric to lie flat. Convex curves, or curves that go out do not require clipping.

❖ Sew the pieces that "tuck under" another piece first, for example, sew the stems first. Next, sew the flower or leaf that covers the end of the stem.

❖ Using the point and edge of your needle, turn under the fabric on the drawn seam line and appliqué the shape into the background fabric. Try to achieve about 7-9 stitches per inch.

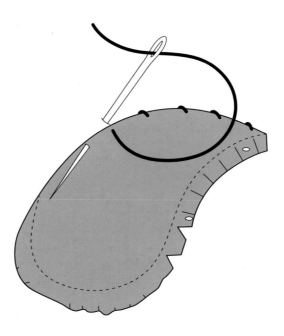

A screened-in porch provides the perfect area to display vintage plates, favorite finds and stamped samplers found in flea markets. Joy looks for old frames at Goodwill and estate sales. These are painted, sanded and reused to frame her samplers.

Joy's Home

*Joy Hayward balances a stressful career
with a calm found stitching samplers*

Joy Hayward needed a respite from her stressful real estate job. A lunch break at the local
stitchery shop provided this and more. The colors of the floss and the variety of patterns in
the shop were seductive. She purchased her first cross-stitch project that day and began stitching that evening. It became a life-long passion for Joy. That first project was stitched on 18-
count Aida fabric. Later the shop owner convinced her to try linen. Once Joy learned to stitch
on linen, it became her fabric of choice.

Her husband, Jim, had an aunt who loved antiques and shared this interest with Joy. As Joy
began to encounter antique samplers, her appreciation for them grew. She couldn't spend the
money required to purchase an antique, so Joy began stitching reproduction samplers. Some of
her reproduction samplers have been artificially aged. Joy rubs some areas on the linen with
sandpaper and overdyes the linen with tan dye to give them an aged look. After getting such
great results from this technique, Joy cautions us to be very careful when purchasing any
antique sampler.

As you begin to look through Joy's home, you see the results of her many years of stitching.
Above an antique dry sink, a grouping of reproduction cross-stitch samplers commands your
attention as you enter her home.

After Christmas each year, Joy begins choosing and planning her next large project. Each
New Year's Day is anticipated and celebrated by stitching her next sampler.

ABOVE: Not all samplers are individually framed. This small sampler was placed with favorite family pictures and letters. RIGHT: A favorite sampler takes the most prominent position in the house, right above the fireplace, and Joy changes them with the seasons. This one celebrates Christmas. Annie, Joy's cat, enjoys this cozy setting.

ABOVE: Antique wooden bowls hold a project in progress. LEFT: A secret fairy garden creates a magical setting on her dining table, perfect to entertain her granddaughter. RIGHT: The bedroom is easily transformed to await a visit from a special granddaughter. Each of the samplers on the wall were stitched by Joy.

ABOVE: Tucked away on a shelf inside a cabinet, a Christmas sampler marks the season. RIGHT: As you enter Joy's home, the samplers positioned above an antique dry sink command your attention.

Design by Barb Adams • Sewing by Leona Adams • Quilting by Jeanne Zyck

Charmingly Yours

PROJECT SIZE: 31 ½" x 31 ½"

INSTRUCTIONS

Cut the appliqué block 21 1/2" x 21 1/2" from the brown and pink print.

❖ Make templates of the appliqué shapes. Refer to the template pages and cut out the pieces needed for the block.

❖ Use the Clover bias tape maker and make 42" of 1/4" bias tape from a teal print.

❖ Refer to the placement diagram and position the pieces on the background block.

❖ Baste the pieces on the block and appliqué them in place.

❖ Set the appliqué block aside.

BORDER

❖ Cut squares from the charm pack twice diagonally.

❖ Mix the triangles. Pick up 2 dark and 2 light triangles. Sew them together to create one square block. Refer to the diagram.

❖ Repeat for 45 pieced blocks. The finished size of each pieced block is 3 1/2".

❖ Refer to the picture and sew the quilt top together.

Supply List

❖ 1 "Chelsea Boutique" Charm Pack by Blackbird Designs for Moda fabrics
❖ 1 yd. brown and pink print for the appliqué block and binding
❖ Fat quarter each of 2 pink prints
❖ Fat quarter each of 3 teal prints
❖ 1/4" Clover bias tape maker

Placement Diagram - Each square = 1"

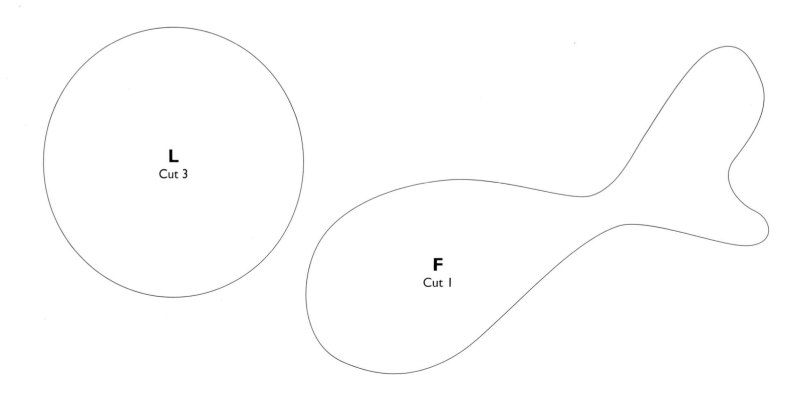

L
Cut 3

F
Cut 1

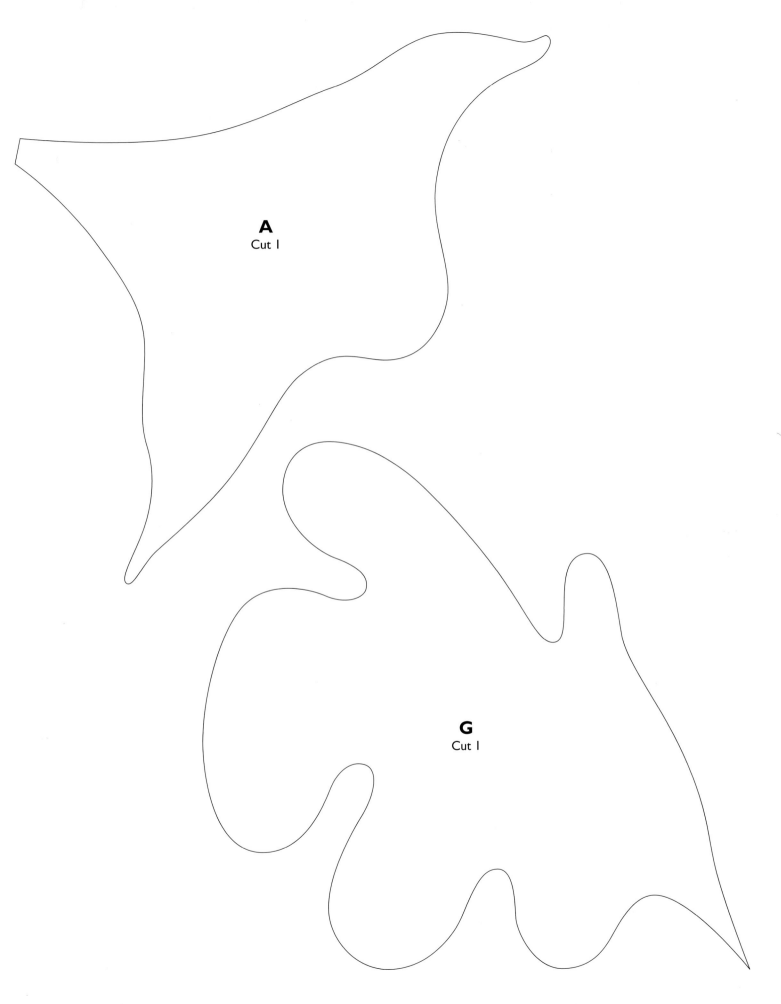

A
Cut 1

G
Cut 1

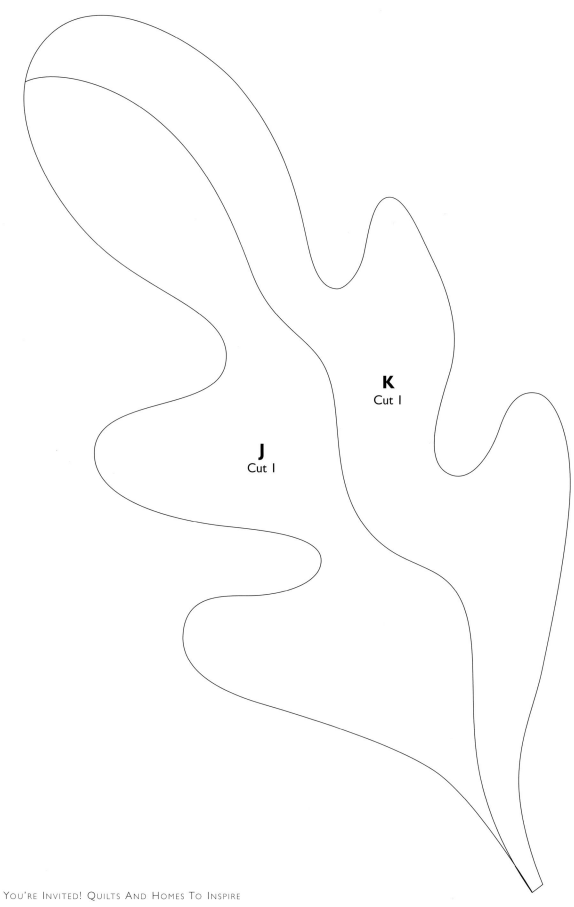

K
Cut 1

J
Cut 1

B
Cut 1

C
Cut 1

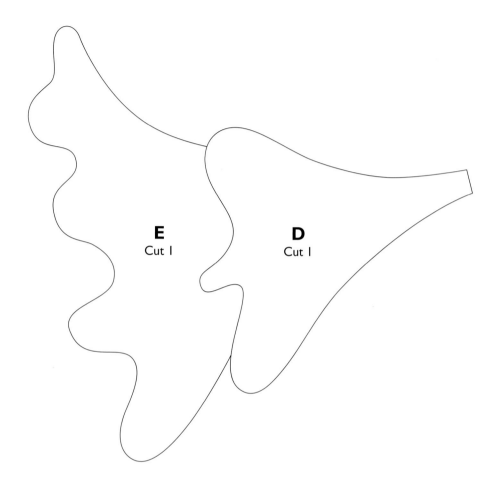

E
Cut 1

D
Cut 1

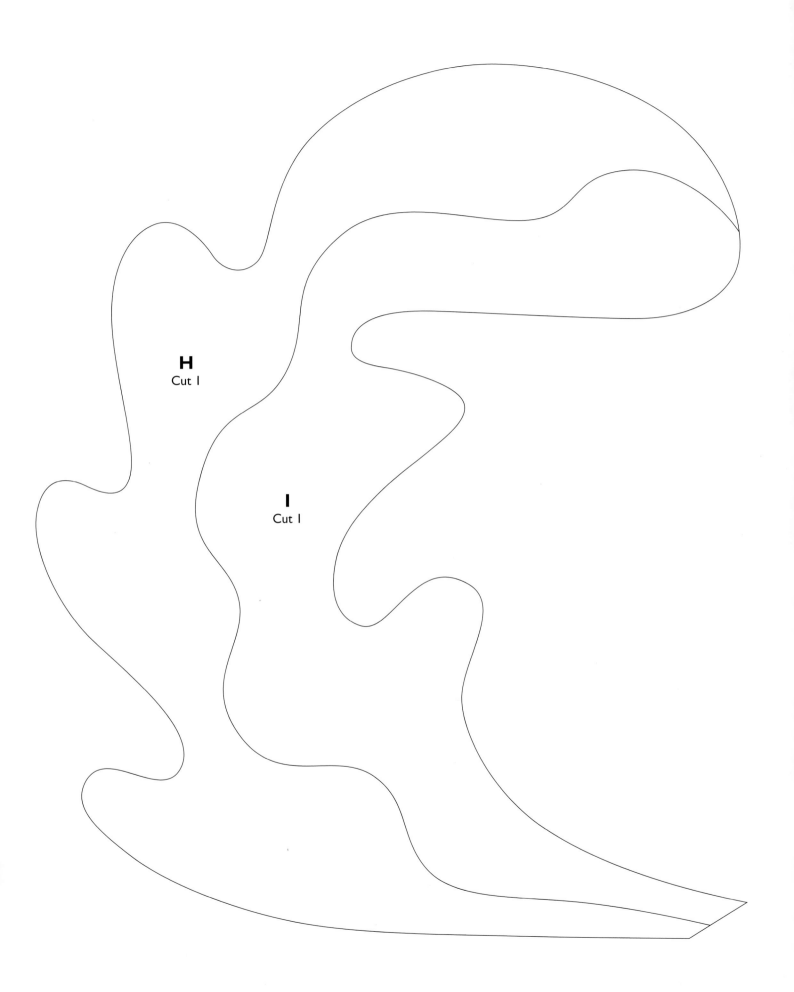

H
Cut 1

I
Cut 1

Design by Barb Adams • Sewing by Leona Adams • Quilting by Jeanne Zyck

Oh Baby, Baby!

PROJECT SIZE: 40" x 40"

INSTRUCTIONS

❖ Cut 400 – 2 1/2" squares from light prints.

❖ Cut 400 – 2 1/2" squares from dark prints.

❖ Place one light square and one dark square right sides together. Sew a seam along the diagonal as illustrated in Diagram A.

Diagram A

❖ Trim away the excess fabric as illustrated in Diagram B.

Diagram B

❖ Open the half-square triangle units as illustrated in Diagram C and press. Repeat for 400 units.

Diagram C

❖ Sort the units into color families and sew 20 strips of 20 half-square triangle units each as illustrated in Diagram D.

❖ Refer to the picture and sew the 20 strips together.

Diagram D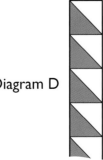

Supply List
❖ 1 "Folkloric" Jellyroll by Fig Tree Quilts for Moda fabrics
❖ Fat quarter each of 3 light prints
❖ 1/3 yd. of a red print for binding

Design by Barb Adams • Sewing by Leona Adams • Quilting by Jeanne Zyck

Winter Holly

PROJECT SIZE: 28" x 28"

INSTRUCTIONS

Cutting measurements include a 1/4" seam allowance.

PIECED BLOCKS

❖ Cut 12 – 2" squares from light tan prints.

❖ Cut 12 – 2 3/8" squares from red prints.

❖ Cut 12 – 2 3/8" squares from green prints.

❖ Cut 12 – 2 3/8" squares from light tan prints.

❖ Place one square each of the green and red print fabric right sides together. Fold the fabric squares in half on the diagonal. Refer to the diagram and sew a 1/4" seam allowance away from the folded edge. Repeat for the remaining side. Cut the pieces apart on the fold line. The results will be two half-square triangle units.

❖ Repeat this process for:
12 red/green, half-square triangle units;
12 red/tan, half-square triangle units;
12 green/tan, half-square triangle units.

❖ Refer to the pieced block sewing diagram and piece three star blocks.

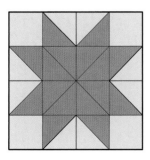

Supply List
The fabric numbers below refer to "Nell's Flower Shop" line of fabric by Blackbird Designs for Moda Fabrics.

❖ 1/2 yd. light tan toile #2581-13
❖ Fat quarter of a light tan print #2586-13
❖ Fat quarter each of 3 different red fabrics #2580-12, 2587-12 and 1712-14
❖ 1/3 yd. green print
❖ Fat quarter dark green print
❖ 1/4" Clover bias tape maker

TWO HOLLY BERRY BLOCKS

❖ Cut 5 - 6 1/2" squares from light prints. Set 3 aside.

❖ Make 2 3/4 yds. of 1/4" bias tape from the green print for the stems. Cut the tape needed for the holly blocks and set aside the remaining bias tape.

❖ Cut out the holly and berry shapes, adding a 1/8" - 1/4" seam allowance. Refer to the diagram and baste the pieces in place on the background fabric.

❖ Appliqué the pieces to the background.

❖ Refer to the picture and sew the holly berry blocks to two star blocks.

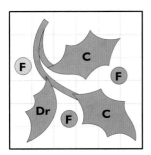

Placement Diagram
Each square = 1"

APPLIQUÉ BLOCK A

❖ Pick up the 3 remaining 6 1/2" squares. Refer to the diagram and sew them together with the remaining star block.

❖ Cut out the shapes for this block, adding a 1/8" - 1/4" seam allowance. Refer to the diagram for Appliqué block A and baste the pieces in place on the background fabric.

❖ Appliqué the pieces to the background.

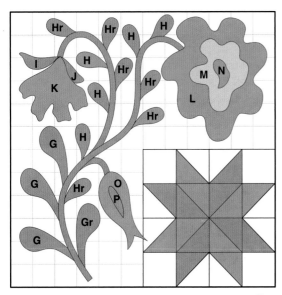

Placement Diagram - Each square = 1"

APPLIQUÉ BLOCK B

❖ Cut 2 – 12 1/2" squares from a light tan print. Set one aside.

❖ Cut out the shapes for this block, adding a 1/8" – 1/4" seam allowance. Refer to the diagram and baste the pieces in place on the background fabric. Note the design is reversed on the second square. Fold the 1/4" bias tape in half for the bird legs.

❖ Appliqué the pieces to the background.

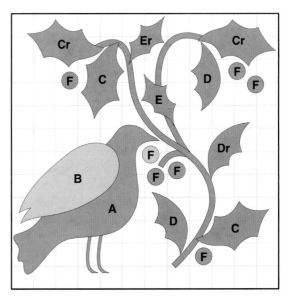

Placement Diagram - Each square = 1"

JOINING BLOCKS

❖ Refer to the picture and sew the four blocks together.

BORDER

❖ Cut 26 – 2 7/8" squares from the light tan print.

❖ Cut 26 – 2 7/8" squares from the red prints.

❖ Make 52 half-square triangle units from the light tan and red prints using the same method illustrated earlier in these instructions.

❖ Sew 2 strips of 12 units each. Refer to the picture for placement of the units. Sew one strip to each side of the quilt.

❖ Sew 2 strips of 14 units each. Refer to the picture for placement of the units. Sew one strip to the top and one to the bottom of the quilt.

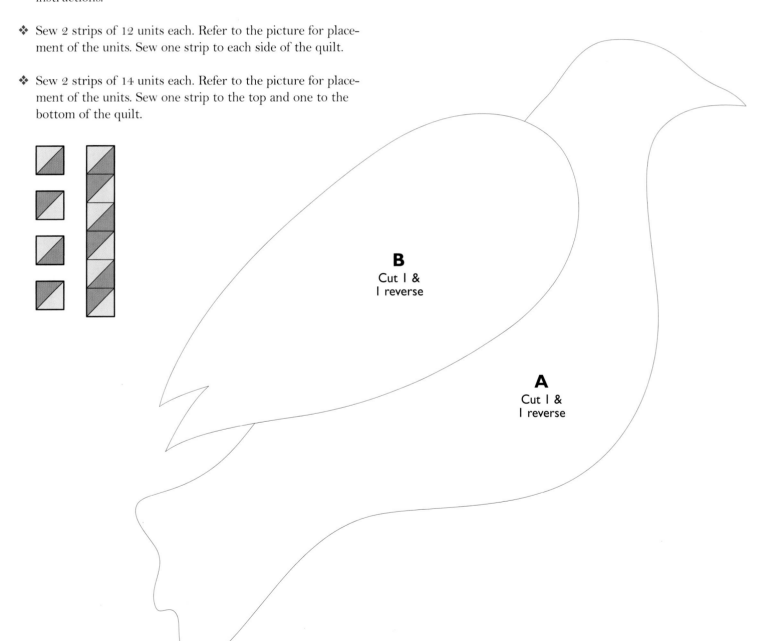

B
Cut 1 &
1 reverse

A
Cut 1 &
1 reverse

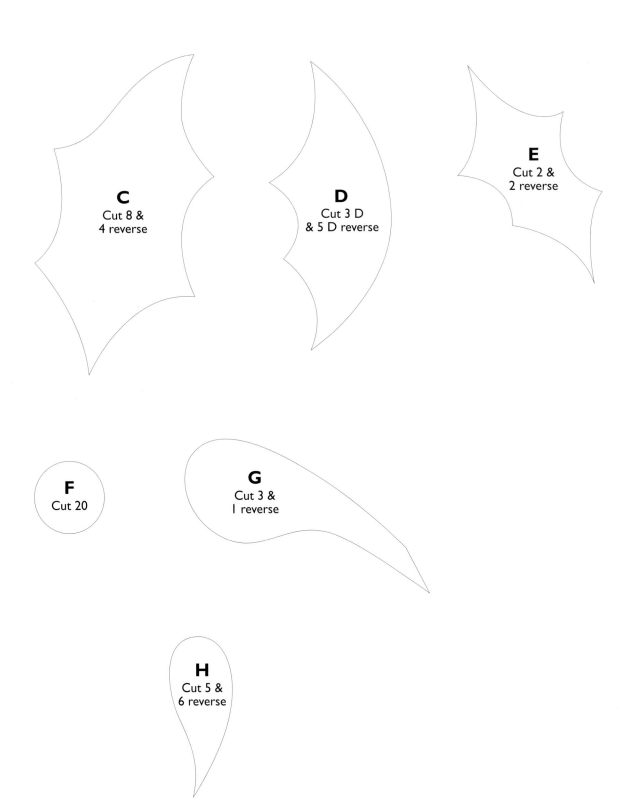

C
Cut 8 &
4 reverse

D
Cut 3 D
& 5 D reverse

E
Cut 2 &
2 reverse

F
Cut 20

G
Cut 3 &
1 reverse

H
Cut 5 &
6 reverse

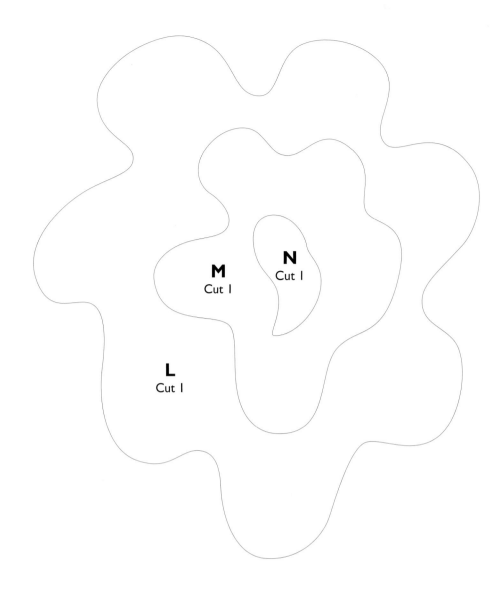

M
Cut 1

N
Cut 1

L
Cut 1

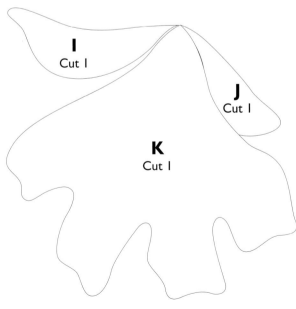

I
Cut 1

J
Cut 1

K
Cut 1

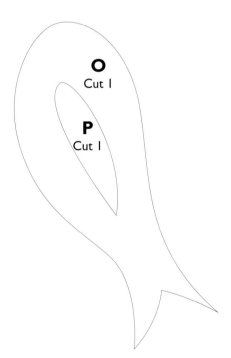

O
Cut 1

P
Cut 1

Design by Alma Allen • Stitched by Alma Allen • Sampler Graphics by Alissa Christianson

Lydia Mitzel Sampler

DESIGN SIZE: 132W x 98H • SAMPLER SIZE: 7¹¹/₁₆" x 5⅝"

Lydia Mitzel is a great-great-great grandmother of mine. She was born in Pennsylvania and moved with her family to Ohio when she was 9 years old.

My daughter Laura turned 21 this summer. I stitched the year 1845 in this sampler because it's the year Lydia turned 21.

After the framing was completed, I put a label on the back of the piece with some information about my grandmother to insure she will not be forgotten.

SYMBOLS

◆ Belle Soie – Cinnamon Stick (DMC 433, 434)

X Belle Soie – Attic Tea (DMC 733, 829)

O Au Ver A Soie 4221 (DMC 738)

● Belle Soie – Chester's Blue (DMC 3762)

INSTRUCTIONS

❖ Cross-stitch with 1 strand of silk floss over 2 linen threads throughout unless noted.

❖ Use the numbers and alphabet provided to personalize your sampler.

❖ Use 1 strand of floss over 1 linen thread for the date and text "forget me not." Use the tent stitch or cross stitch.

❖ Use 1 strand of Au Ver A Soie 4221 for the satin stitch inside the flowers.

❖ Use 1 strand of Cinnamon Stick and stitch the chocolate flowers with the button hole stitch.

Supply List

Belle Soie – Crescent Colours Silk Floss
❖ Belle Soie – Cinnamon Stick (DMC 433, 434)
❖ Belle Soie – Attic Tea (DMC 733, 829)
❖ Au Ver A Soie 4221 (DMC 738)
❖ Belle Soie – Chester's Blue (DMC 3762)
Fabric: 35ct Park City Blend by R & R Reproductions

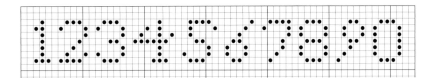

Tent stitch diagram

Maggie's Home

*A vintage home becomes
a couple's haven for their creativity*

The door pictured on the cover of this book welcomes you into Maggie Bonanomi's home. As you enter, you feel as if you have stepped back in time. Built in the 1840's, this Lexington, Missouri home is the perfect backdrop for her collections and artwork.

Peeling paint and cracks in the plaster are part of the vintage touches that Maggie loves. She and her husband, Harold, sleep on an old rope bed, which provides all the comfort they need. Lighting throughout the house is soft and the fixtures create a vintage look. Maggie draws and paints and is not afraid to expand her canvas to her walls. The upstairs fireplace provides a frame for one of her works. Harold, with a twinkle in his eye, says he is always busy with a project, making Maggie's wishes come true.

Vintage linens, quilts and fabrics are hung throughout. The added texture and color of these textiles create backdrops for Maggie's collections. Maggie loves the look and feel of small antique books. She stacks them on shelves and tables waiting to be read.

Maggie's collections and designs take the center stage in her home. She has designed hooked rugs, whimsical journals, penny mats, quilts and cross-stitch. Her work has been featured in many publications.

"Country Sunshine" covers Maggie's antique bed. Topiaries positioned throughout the house reflect Maggie's love of nature.

ABOVE: The "Chelsea Cottage" quilt draws your eye into this cozy bedroom filled with soft textiles. RIGHT: Bathed in light, "In Mollie's Garden" waits to be folded.

Design by Barb Adams • Fabric selection and sewing by Debbie Roberts • Quilting by Heidi Herring

Chelsea Cottage

PROJECT SIZE: 60" x 76"

INSTRUCTIONS

Cutting measurements include a 1/4" seam allowance.
Log Cabin Blocks: 8" square finished

❖ Cut 29 – 2 1/2" pink squares.

❖ Cut 29 each of the following sizes from the light prints.
  A 2 1/2" x 1 1/2"
  B 3 1/2" x 1 1/2"
  E 4 1/2" x 1 1/2"
  F 5 1/2" x 1 1/2"
  I 6 1/2" x 1 1/2"
  J 7 1/2" x 1 1/2"

❖ Cut 29 each of the following sizes from the dark prints.
  C 3 1/2" x 1 1/2"
  D 4 1/2" x 1 1/2"
  G 5 1/2" x 1 1/2"
  H 6 1/2" x 1 1/2"
  K 7 1/2" x 1 1/2"
  L 8 1/2" x 1 1/2"

❖ Starting with the pink squares, sew the logs to the block as shown in the diagram.

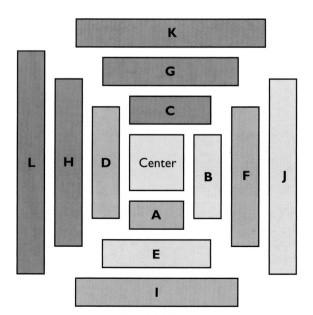

Make 29 Blocks

Supply List
❖ 2 1/2 yds. large-scale brown floral print for the borders and binding
❖ 1 yd. brown and sage plaid for the triangle borders and roof
❖ 1/6 yd. each of 10 light prints for log cabin blocks
❖ 1/6 yd. each of 10 dark prints for log cabin blocks
❖ 1/4 yd. pink floral for the log cabin centers and the flower appliqués
❖ Fat quarter of a light print for the appliqué block
❖ 5/8 yd. of a different light print for the appliqué block
❖ Fat quarter of a green stripe for the vines
❖ 6 1/2" square of a brown print for the steps
❖ 6 1/2" square of a green & brown check for the steps
❖ 6 1/2" square of a light print for the window panes
❖ 10 1/2" square of a red print for the doors and windows
❖ 10 1/2" square of a polka dot print for the dormers
❖ 10 1/2" square of a pink plaid for the dormer gables and heart on the door
❖ 10 1/2" square of a green floral print for the leaves
❖ 1/2" Clover bias tape maker

CENTER HOUSE BLOCK: 16" X 24" FINISHED

❖ Cut 1 – 16 1/2" x 20 1/2" rectangle for the upper background section.

❖ Cut 1 – 16 1/2" x 4 1/2" rectangle for the lower background section.

❖ Sew the two sections together to form a rectangle 16 1/2" x 24 1/2".

❖ Cut 1 – 6" x 11" rectangle for the house.

❖ Cut 1 – 2" x 4 1/2" rectangle for the door.

❖ Cut 2 – 2" x 3" rectangles for the downstairs windows.

❖ Cut 2 – 1 1/4" x 2 1/4" rectangles for the downstairs window panes.

❖ Cut 2 – 2" x 2 1/4" rectangles for the upstairs windows.

❖ Cut 2 – 1 1/4" x 1 3/4" rectangles for the upstairs windowpanes.

❖ Cut 1 – 1 1/4" x 3 1/2" rectangle for the largest step.

❖ Cut 2 – 1 1/4" x 2" rectangles for the smaller steps.

❖ Cut 2 – 1 3/4" x 2 1/4" rectangles for the chimneys.

❖ Make 27" of 1/2" bias vine.

❖ Make templates of the appliqué shapes. Refer to the template page and cut out the pieces needed for the block.

❖ Refer to the placement diagram and position the pieces on the background block.

❖ Baste the pieces on the block and appliqué them in place.

❖ Refer to the diagram and sew the log cabin blocks and appliqué block together to form the quilt top.

BORDERS

❖ Cut 29 – 5 1/4" squares of brown floral fabric for the border triangles. Cut each square in half twice on the diagonal.

- Cut 29 – 5 1/4" squares of brown and sage plaid for the border triangles. Cut each square in half twice on the diagonal.

- Sew 2 strips each of 14 brown floral and 15 plaid border triangles. Sew one strip to each side of the quilt top beginning and ending the seam 1/4" from the ends to allow for mitering.

- Sew 2 strips each of 10 brown floral and 11 plaid border triangles. Sew one strip each to the top and bottom of the quilt top beginning and ending the seam 1/4" from the ends to allow for mitering.

- Sew the sage plaid triangles together at each corner to complete mitering.

- Cut 2 borders each 6 1/2" x 60 1/2" from the large-scale brown floral. Sew one to each side of the quilt top.

- Cut 2 borders each 6 1/2" x 56 1/2" from the large-scale brown floral. Sew one each to the top and bottom of the quilt top.

- Sew 2 strips each of 19 brown floral and 18 plaid border triangles. Sew one strip to each side of the quilt top beginning and ending the seam 1/4" from the ends to allow for mitering.

- Sew 2 strips each of 15 brown floral and 14 plaid border triangles. Sew one each to the top and bottom of the quilt top beginning and ending the seam 1/4" from the end to allow for mitering.

- Sew the brown floral triangles together at each corner to complete mitering.

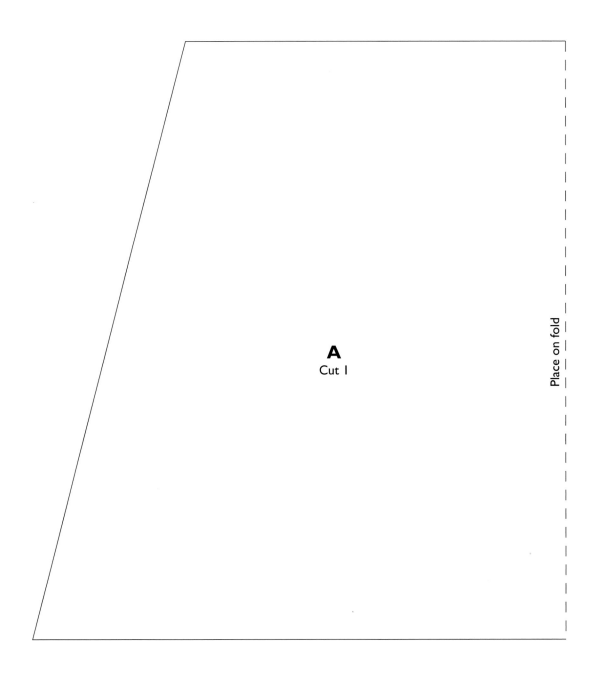

A
Cut 1

Place on fold

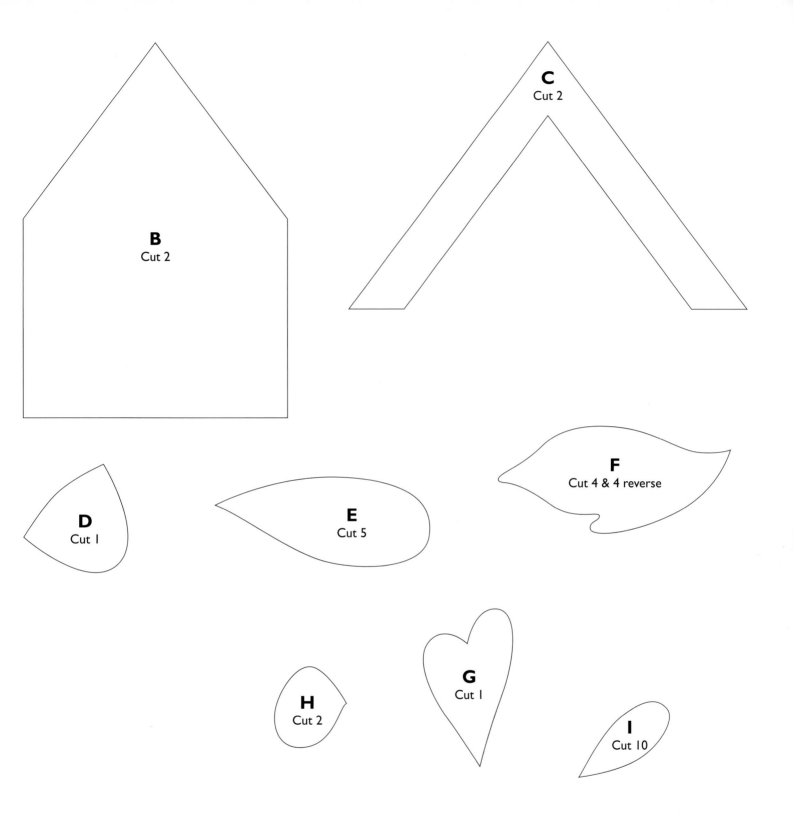

B
Cut 2

C
Cut 2

D
Cut 1

E
Cut 5

F
Cut 4 & 4 reverse

H
Cut 2

G
Cut 1

I
Cut 10

Design and sewing by Lorraine Hofmann • Quilting by Jeanne Zyck

Country Sunshine

PROJECT SIZE: 92" x 92"

INSTRUCTIONS

Cutting measurements include a 1/4" seam allowance.

APPLIQUÉ BLOCK A (CORNER BLOCKS)

Placement Diagram - Each square = 1"

❖ Cut 4 – 20 1/2" squares from an assortment of butter-yellow background prints.

❖ Refer to the placement diagram and note the templates needed for this block. Refer to the template pages and make the templates of the appliqué shapes. Cut out the pieces needed for each block.

❖ Use the Clover bias tape maker and make 10 2/3 yds. of 1/2" bias tape from an assortment of golden brown prints. This will be enough bias tape for all 4 blocks.

❖ Refer to the placement diagram and position the pieces on each background block.

❖ Baste the pieces on the block and appliqué them in place.

❖ Set the appliqué blocks aside.

Supply List

❖ 3/4 yd. each of 3 butter-yellows for backgrounds and border triangles
❖ 1 1/2 yd. each of 3 butter-yellows for backgrounds and border triangles
❖ 3 yd. of another butter-yellow for borders
❖ 1 fat quarter of a brown floral for the baskets
❖ 5 – 7 fat quarters of greens for flower sepals & leaves
❖ 5 – 7 fat quarters of golden brown prints for vines
❖ 1 yd. additional of one of the golden brown prints for the border vines
❖ 1/3 yd. each of 6 red/pink prints for flowers and border triangles
❖ 1 yd. additional of one of the red prints for the binding
❖ 5 fat quarters (or scraps) of purple prints for berries
❖ Scraps of rusty/dark red prints for flower stigmas
❖ 1/2" Clover bias tape maker

Cross-stitch supplies
❖ 5" square of 25ct. Yellow Dublin Linen for the center of middle block (if you choose to cross-stitch your initials and date on the quilt)
❖ Scrap of solid yellow fabric to back the linen
❖ DMC floss #820
❖ Tapestry needle

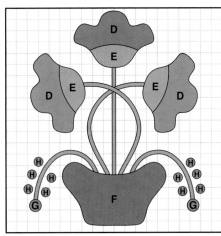

Placement Diagram - Each square = 1"

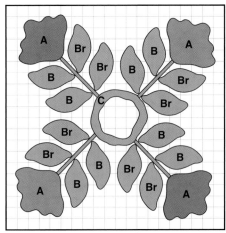

Placement Diagram - Each square = 1"

APPLIQUÉ BLOCK B (SIDE BLOCKS)

❖ Cut 4 - 20 1/2" squares from an assortment of butter-yellow background prints.

❖ Refer to the placement diagram and note the templates needed for this block. Refer to the template pages and make the templates of the appliqué shapes. Cut out the pieces needed for each block.

❖ Use the Clover bias tape maker and make 5 yds. of 1/2" bias tape from an assortment of golden brown prints. This will be enough bias tape for all 4 side blocks.

❖ Refer to the placement diagram and position the pieces on the background block.

❖ Baste the pieces on the block and appliqué them in place.

❖ Set the appliqué blocks aside.

APPLIQUÉ BLOCK C (CENTER BLOCK)

❖ Stitch your initials and date on the yellow linen. Refer to the cross-stitch graph on page 49. Stitch over 2 linen threads with 2 strands of DMC floss. Set the stitched linen piece aside.

❖ Cut 1 – 20 1/2" square from a butter-yellow background print.

❖ Refer to the placement diagram and note the templates needed for this block. Refer to the template pages and make the templates of the appliqué shapes. Cut out the pieces needed for the block.

❖ Use the Clover bias tape maker and make 22" of 1/2" bias tape from a golden brown print.

❖ Refer to the placement diagram and position the pieces on the background block. Center the stitched piece under Template C and baste in place.

❖ Baste the remaining pieces on the block and appliqué them in place.

❖ Refer to the picture and sew the blocks together.

PIECED BORDER

❖ Cut 38 – 5 1/4" squares from the various red/pink prints. Cut each square in half on the diagonal twice, resulting in 152 triangles.

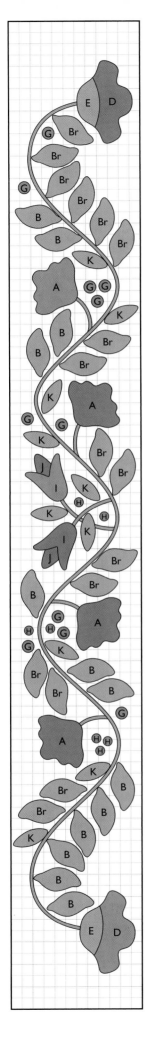

Placement Diagram - Each square = 1"

- ❖ Cut 36 − 5 1/4" squares from the various butter-yellow prints. Cut each square in half on the diagonal twice, resulting in 144 triangles.

- ❖ Cut 2 − 4 7/8" squares from one of the butter-yellow prints. Cut each square in half once on the diagonal. These will be the corner triangles.

- ❖ Refer to the picture and sew 4 strips each of 15 red/pink triangles and 14 yellow triangles. Sew one strip to the top, one strip to the bottom and one to each side of the quilt, with the base of the red triangles toward the center.

- ❖ Fold the corner triangles in half to find the center. Align this fold with the center of the corner. Pin and sew in place. Repeat for the 3 remaining corners.

APPLIQUÉ BORDER

- ❖ Cut 2 border strips 12 1/2" x 64 1/2" from a butter-yellow print. Sew one strip to each side of the quilt top.

- ❖ Cut 2 border strips 12 1/2" x 88 1/2" from a butter-yellow print. These will be the top and bottom borders.

- ❖ Refer to the placement diagram and note the templates needed for the borders. Cut out the pieces needed for the borders.

- ❖ Use the Clover bias tape maker and make 12 1/2 yds. of 1/2" bias tape from a golden brown print. This will be enough bias tape for all 4 appliqué borders.

- ❖ Refer to the placement diagram and position the pieces along the top border.

- ❖ Baste the pieces on the top border strip and appliqué them in place. Repeat for the bottom border.

- ❖ Sew the top border and bottom border in place.

- ❖ Refer to the placement diagram and position the pieces along one side border. Baste and appliqué in place.

- ❖ Repeat for the remaining side border.

FINAL PIECED BORDER

- ❖ Refer to the picture and sew 4 strips each of 21 red/pink triangles and 22 yellow triangles. Sew one strip to the top, one strip to the bottom and one to each side of the quilt, with the base of the red triangles facing to the outside of the quilt top.

- ❖ Sew 2 of the remaining red triangles together to form a corner triangle. Repeat until you have 4 corner triangles. Sew one corner triangle to each corner of the quilt top to finish.

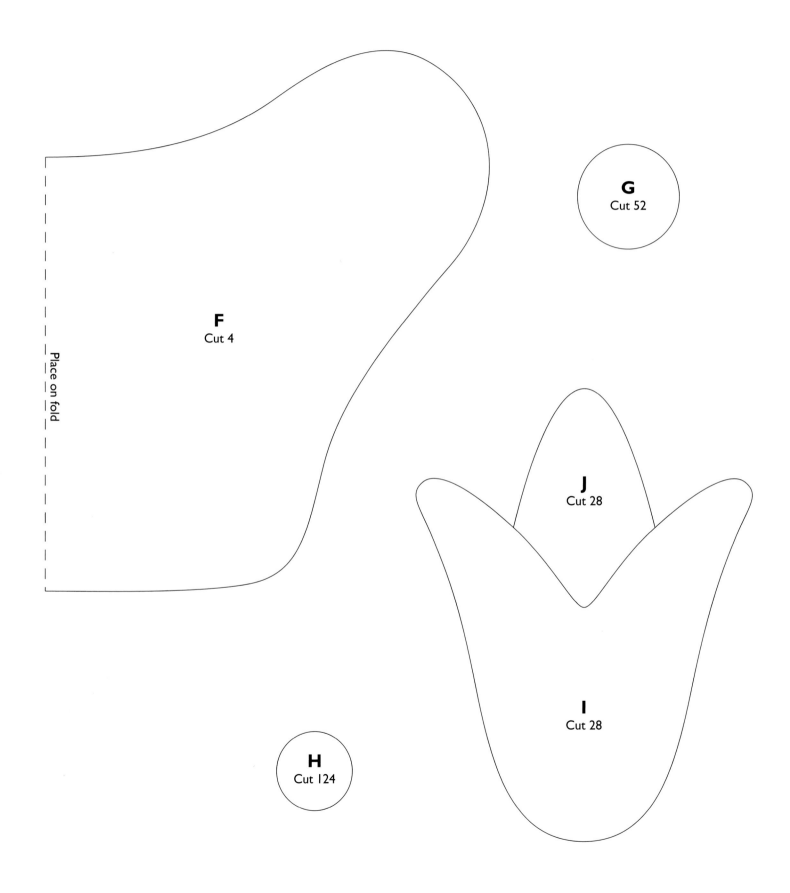

Place on fold

F
Cut 4

G
Cut 52

J
Cut 28

I
Cut 28

H
Cut 124

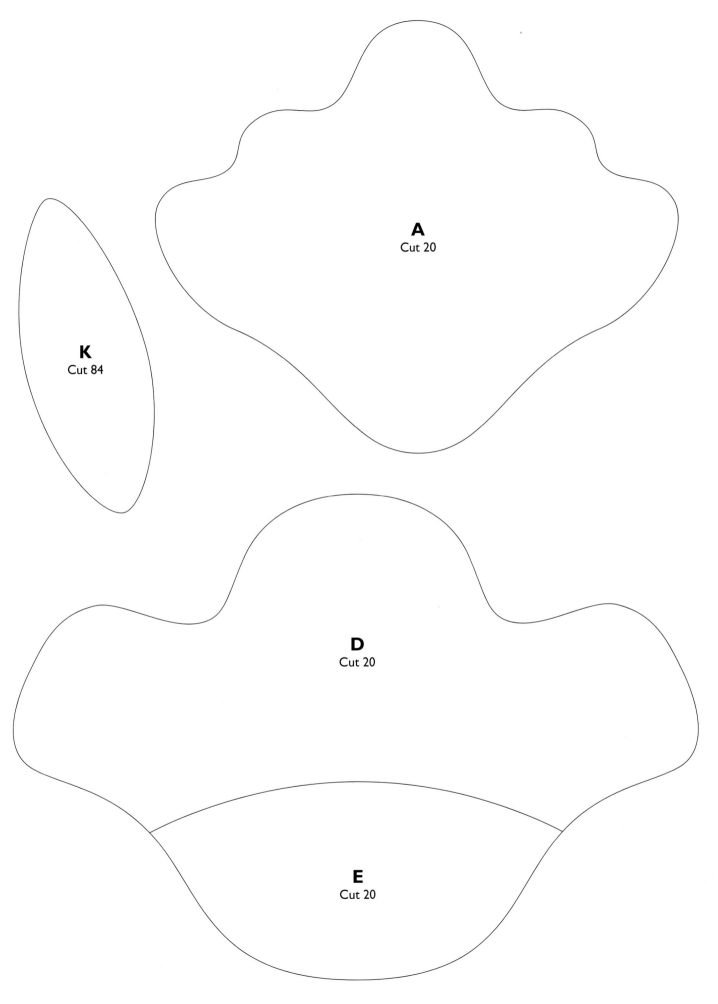

K
Cut 84

A
Cut 20

D
Cut 20

E
Cut 20

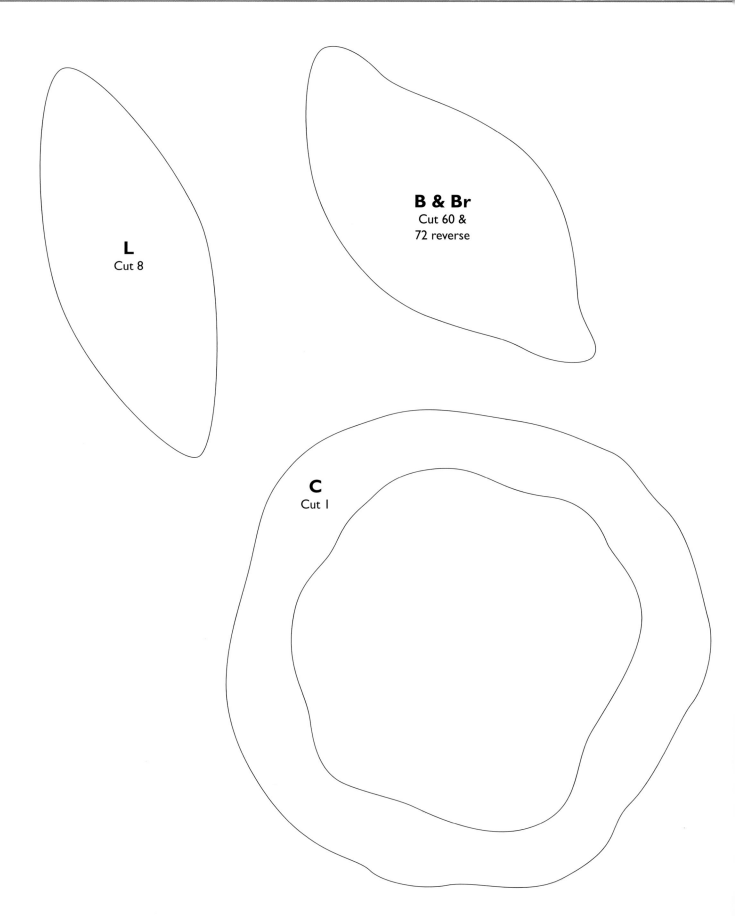

L
Cut 8

B & Br
Cut 60 &
72 reverse

C
Cut 1

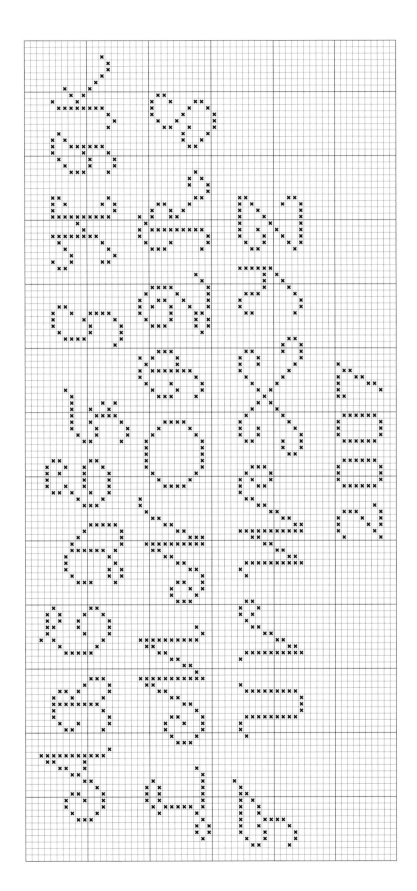

Alphabet Graph to personalize Appliqué Block C (Center block)

Design by Barb Adams • Sewing by Leona Adams • Quilting by Jeanne Zyck

Summer Flags Flying

PROJECT SIZE: 32" x 38"

INSTRUCTIONS

Cutting measurements include a 1/4" seam allowance.

❖ Sort the 5" charm squares into a pile of light prints and a pile of dark prints.

❖ Make a template for piece H. Cut out one piece H from a dark print from the charm squares. Refer to the diagram below and center the dark circle on a light print square.

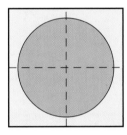

❖ Appliqué the circle in place. Repeat for 13 dark circles on light backgrounds and 7 light circles on dark backgrounds.

❖ Refer to the diagram and cut each square in half twice. The results will be 4 − 2 1/2" squares.

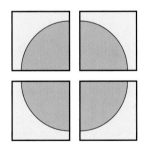

❖ Refer to the placement diagram and sew the squares together to form the center of the quilt top.

Supply List

Reference numbers for Moda Fabric "Madeira" provided below:

❖ 1"Madeira"Charm Pack by Blackbird Designs for Moda fabrics
❖ 1 yd. of a light print for borders and border triangles (2607-15)
❖ Fat quarter each of 3 red prints for berries, flag, bias vine, leaves and border triangles (2600-13, 2602-13 and 2606-12)
❖ Fat quarter each of 2 blue prints for leaves, berries, border triangles and flag (2601-14 and 2608-14)
❖ Fat quarter of a brown print for the flag poles (2602-12)
❖ Fat quarter each of 2 green prints for the leaves (2605-15 2601-15)
❖ 1/4" Clover bias tape maker

Placement Diagram

- Cut 2 strips 6 1/2" x 20 1/2" from the light fabric. Sew one strip to each side of the quilt top.

- Cut 1 strips 6 1/2" x 28 1/2" from the light fabric. Sew the strip to the top of the quilt top.

- Cut 1 strips 8 1/2" x 28 1/2" from the light fabric. Sew the strip to the bottom of the quilt top.

PIECED BORDER

- Cut 24 – 2 7/8" squares from the red prints.

- Cut 8 – 2 7/8" squares from the blue print.

- Cut 32 – 2 7/8" squares from the light print.

- Cut 4 – 2 1/2" squares from a red print and set these aside.

- Place one square each of the red and light print fabric right sides together. Draw a line along the diagonal, dividing the square in half. Refer to the diagram on page 21 and sew a 1/4" seam allowance away from the drawn line. Repeat for the remaining side. Cut the pieces apart on the drawn line. The results will be two half-square triangle units. Repeat for a total of 64 half-square triangle units. You will need 15 blue units and 47 red units.

- Open the half-square triangle units and press.

- Refer to the placement diagram and note the direction of the half-square triangles. Sew 2 strips of 17 units each. Sew one strip to each side of the quilt top.

- Refer to the placement diagram and note the direction of the half-square triangles. Sew 2 strips of 14 units each. Begin and end each strip with one red square. Sew one strip to the top and and one to the bottom of the quilt top.

- Use the Clover bias tape maker and make 3 yds. of 1/4" bias tape from a red print.

- Refer to the placement diagram and note the templates needed for the borders. Refer to the template pages and make the templates of the appliqué shapes. Cut out the pieces needed.

- Refer to the placement diagram and position the pieces along the borders.

- Baste the pieces and appliqué them in place.

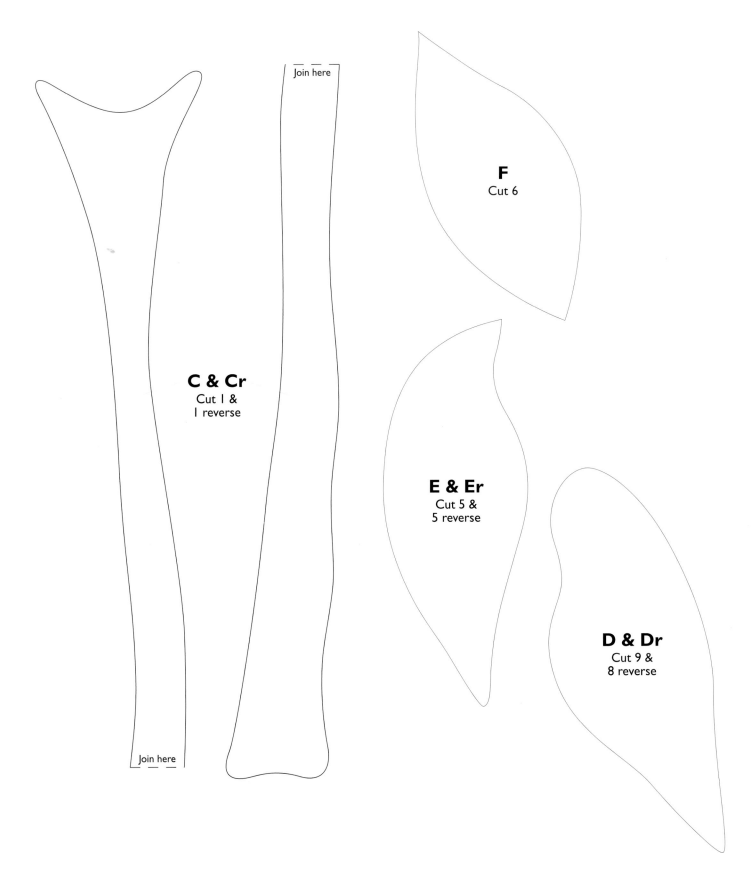

Join here

C & Cr
Cut 1 &
1 reverse

Join here

F
Cut 6

E & Er
Cut 5 &
5 reverse

D & Dr
Cut 9 &
8 reverse

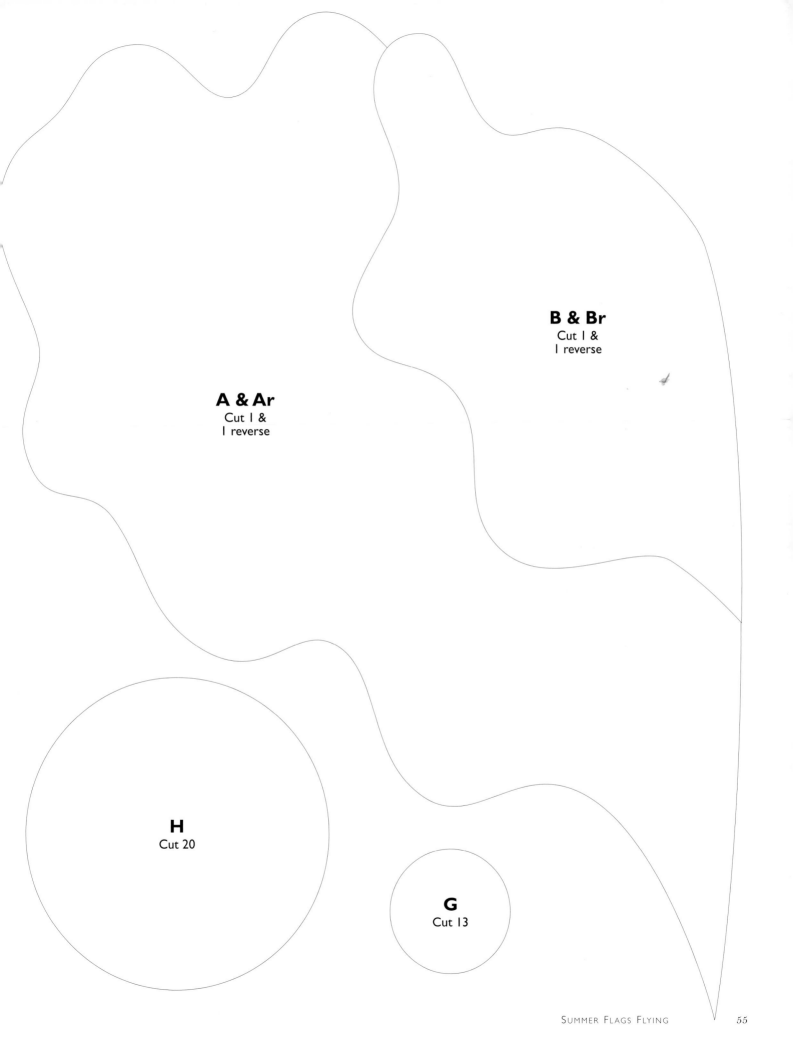

B & Br
Cut 1 &
1 reverse

A & Ar
Cut 1 &
1 reverse

H
Cut 20

G
Cut 13

Design and sewing by Yelena Elliott • Quilting by Susan Campbell

In Mollie's Garden

PROJECT SIZE: 55" x 65"

My Gran, Marie Bloxsom, was known to family and friends as Mollie. The design for this quilt came about one day when I was thinking about all of the things that remind me of her. The world seems a lonely place without this gentle woman. Gran's garden was her pride and joy. Flowers were always blooming in her garden and certain ones evoke strong memories for me, some of these are included in the border appliqué design. The flat four petal rose in rich red, grows on a trellis and was planted in memory of her son, my Uncle Ray.

Certain things could be depended upon with my Gran: red cordial in the fridge door; cake and biscuits in the tub; and rain, hail or shine the driveway always got swept. Hopefully one day when I'm a grandmother, my grandkids will enjoy remembering things about me like I do about my Gran. — *Yelena Elliott*

INSTRUCTIONS

Cutting measurements include a 1/4" seam allowance.

SIGNATURE BLOCK: 100 - 5" BLOCKS

❖ Cut 1 – 1 7/8" square from a tan print for piece A. One is needed for each block.

❖ Cut 4 – 4 1/2" x 1 7/8" rectangles from brown, blue or lavender prints for piece B. Four are needed for each block.

❖ Cut 1 – 4 1/4" square from a light print for piece C. Cut the square twice on the diagonal for 4 triangles. One square is needed for each block.

❖ Refer to Diagram A and sew the pieces together to form the block.

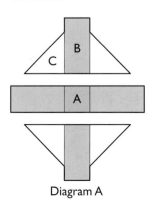

Diagram A

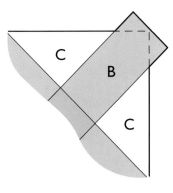

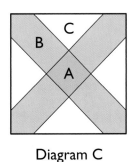

Diagram C

Diagram B

❖ Refer to Diagram B and C and trim the corners.

❖ Cut 180 sashing strips 1" x 5 1/2" from a light print.

❖ Cut 81 corner stones 1" x 1" from a tan print.

❖ Refer to the picture and sew the blocks together with the sashing and corner stones.

APPLIQUÉ BORDER

❖ Cut 1 strip 55" x 10 1/4" from a light cream print.

❖ Make templates of the appliqué shapes. Refer to the template pages and cut out the pieces needed for the border.

❖ Use the Clover bias tape maker and make 4 1/2 yards of 3/8" bias tape from the brown fabrics.

❖ Refer to the placement diagram and whimsically position the pieces on the border strip.

❖ Baste the pieces on the border and appliqué them in place.

❖ Sew the border to the quilt top.

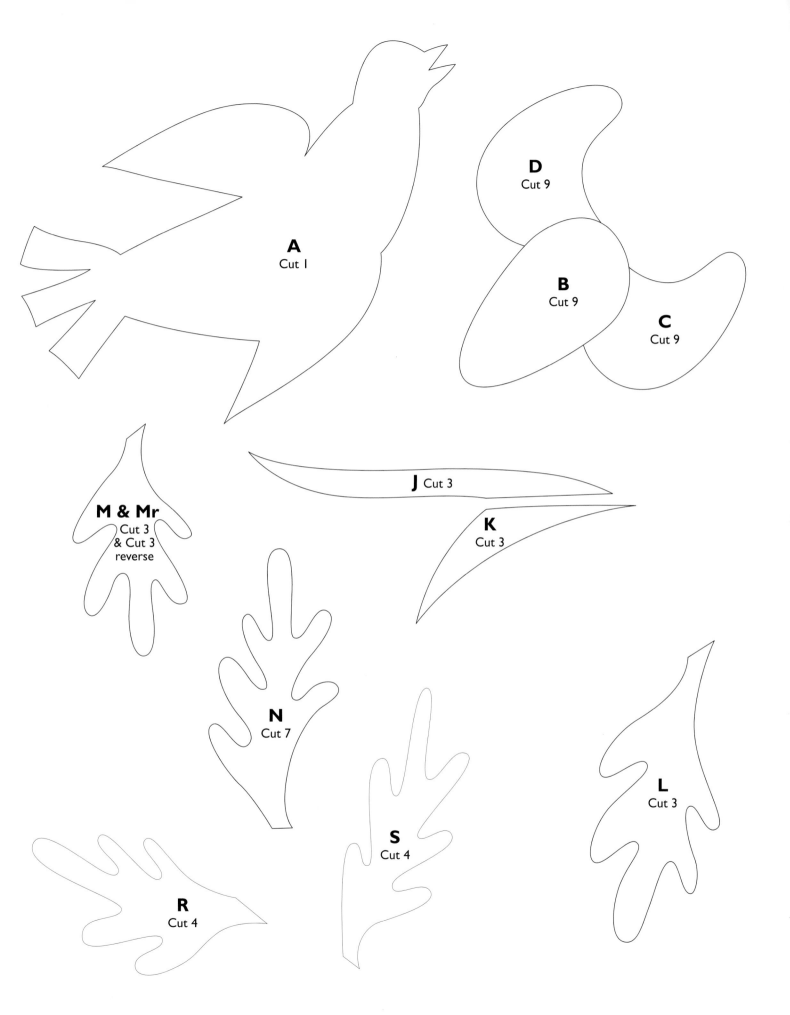

A
Cut 1

D
Cut 9

B
Cut 9

C
Cut 9

J Cut 3

K
Cut 3

M & Mr
Cut 3
& Cut 3
reverse

N
Cut 7

L
Cut 3

S
Cut 4

R
Cut 4

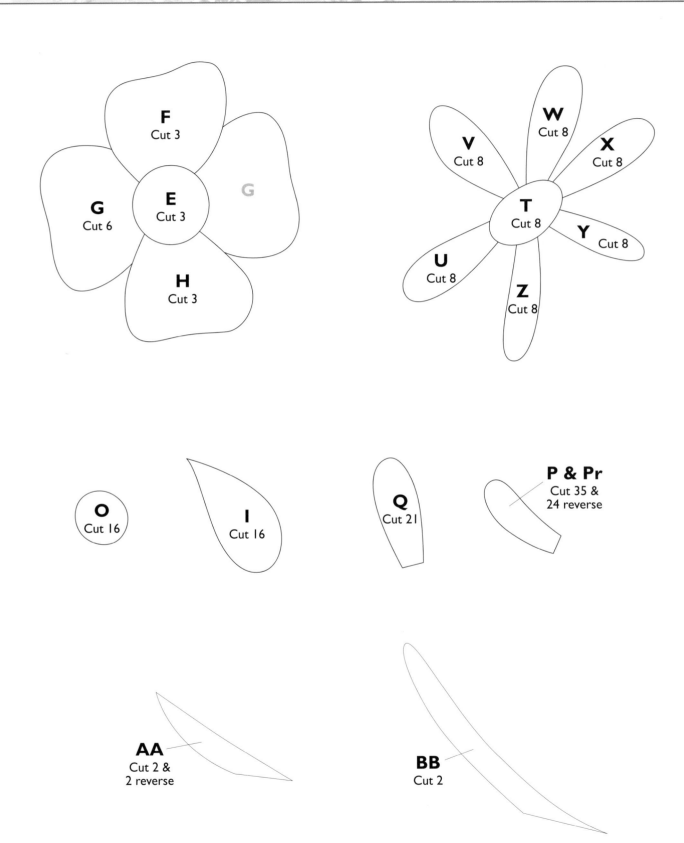

F
Cut 3

G
Cut 6

E
Cut 3

G

H
Cut 3

W
Cut 8

V
Cut 8

X
Cut 8

T
Cut 8

Y
Cut 8

U
Cut 8

Z
Cut 8

O
Cut 16

I
Cut 16

Q
Cut 21

P & Pr
Cut 35 &
24 reverse

AA
Cut 2 &
2 reverse

BB
Cut 2

Placement Diagram - Each square = 1"

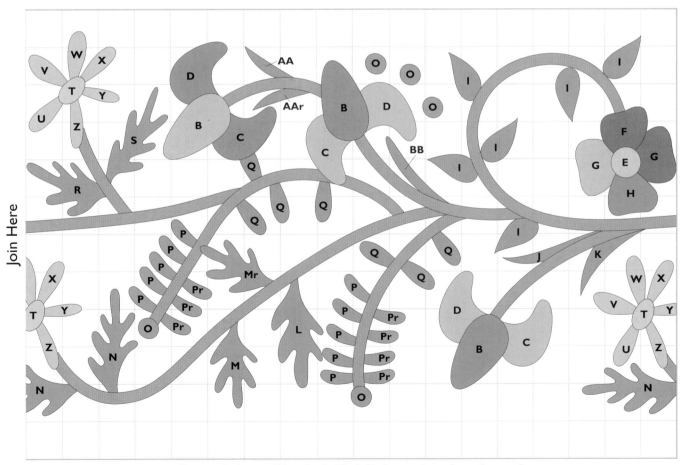

Repeat design until border is filled. (Refer to photo for reference.)

Sara's Home

A son's paintings determine the color palette for his parents' lovely and welcoming home

Tyler Larson began painting at a young age. His parents, Sara and Paul Larson, encouraged his developing artistic abilities. Most of his paintings are done from life, in one sitting. (In French terms, *plein air/á la prima.*) Sara uses his works to set the mood and tone for each room in her home. The light colors on the walls in Sara's home are the perfect gallery to showcase Tyler's paintings. After carefully selecting the painting for each room, she begins to decorate around it, using colors reflected in the piece.

Sara has a wonderful collection of vintage quilts. Their soft colors and patterns add to the casual, welcoming feel of each room. Even outdoors, Sara uses a vintage quilt as a table cover. The pattern of that quilt, Seven Sisters, has always been one of her favorites. The large graphic stars are perfect for a summer day.

Hidden among the flowers in her garden are small stone cottages. These were carved during a class with Miles Schachter, a sculptor in Lawrence, Kansas. Sara loves working with stone and has a large collection of stone waiting for her chisel and hammer. A stone leaf sits on her deck and is used as a bird bath.

Sara hates to see items discarded. Her bedskirts are made from old sweaters she rescued at Goodwill. She included the pockets and buttons in these creations. The pockets are perfect for reading glasses at night.

In Sara's dining room, the dining chairs showcase her fun sense of design. Sara shared the pattern for the chairs with us and it is included in this book.

More of Tyler's work can be seen at www.dreamhouseart.com. If you would like to order one of Sara's unique bedskirts, contact her at sajolarson@aol.com.

Tyler's painting of a carefree afternoon at the pool glows in the light from the living room window. Sara's hooked rugs frame the room.

RIGHT: Drawn from her collection of vintage quilts, "Seven Sisters" serves as a table cover for an outdoor summer gathering. BELOW: Two of Sara's stone carvings: A small cottage and a leaf used as a bird bath add charm to her colorful back yard.

ABOVE: One of Tyler's paintings sets the tone for this inviting bedroom. LEFT: Sweaters bought at Goodwill are stitched together to make a whimsical bedskirt. Pockets and buttons remain as reminders of their past use.

Old red sweaters make up the bed skirt in Sara's room. Their red color is the perfect frame for a quilt she made in a class taught by Kathleen Brassfield.

Design by Sara Larson • Sewing by Sara Larson

Knitted Floral Chair Covers

PROJECT SIZE: VARIES

INSTRUCTIONS

The chair seat

❖ Flip the chair over and remove the screws from underneath the seat. Look carefully for these screws, the cloth covering may hide them. Remove the tacks or staples that hold the old upholstery fabric to the seat, and lift off the fabric. Use it as a template for the new chair covers. If you use the front and back of one black sweater, there will be enough for two "new" covers.

❖ Check the padding to make sure it can be reused. If it's damaged replace it with new padding. Foam padding and cotton padding are available precut for chair seats. You might be able to fluff and smooth old cotton padding; adding a layer of foam padding to build the seat cushion up to 3/4 to 1".

❖ Lay one knitted cover flat, wrong side up, and center the the padded seat on top of it upside down. Fold the edges of the knitted fabric up over the seat, stretching it firmly onto the plywood. Start at the center of one side, and attach it to the seat with a staple gun or flathead upholstery tacks. Set them apart 1 to 1 1/2" along the side of the seat. Check to make sure the fabric is straight, with no wrinkles. Turn the seat over again, and fasten the other sides.

❖ Replace the chair seat in the frame, replace all the screws, and tighten them securely.

Sara hooked a vein in each flower petal with a 1/4" strip of red wool. This detail can be replaced. Use 6 strands of floss and stitch the stem stitch along the line shown on the template. If you wish to use the hooking detail, draw the template on the sweater and hook the vein for the flower petal before cutting out the template.

The flower

❖ Make templates of the flower and leaf shapes. Refer to the template page and cut out the pieces needed for the flower. No seam allowance is needed for these.

❖ Blanket stitch around each petal with 6 strands of DMC

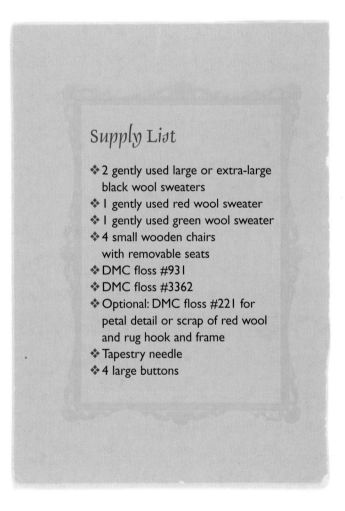

Supply List

❖ 2 gently used large or extra-large black wool sweaters
❖ 1 gently used red wool sweater
❖ 1 gently used green wool sweater
❖ 4 small wooden chairs with removable seats
❖ DMC floss #931
❖ DMC floss #3362
❖ Optional: DMC floss #221 for petal detail or scrap of red wool and rug hook and frame
❖ Tapestry needle
❖ 4 large buttons

#931 floss. Tack the pleats in each petal.

❖ Blanket stitch around each leaf with 6 strands of DMC #3362 floss. Tack the pleat in each leaf.

❖ Position the flower petals, overlapping them a bit and zigzag them together on the sewing machine with matching thread.

❖ Sew the leaves in place on the back of the flower petals.

❖ Use a large old button to cover the center stitching on the flower. Stitch the button in place.

❖ Tack the flower in place on the knitted chair seat.

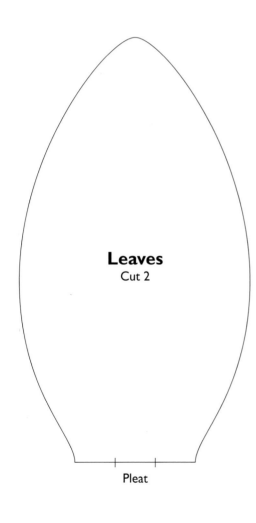

Leaves
Cut 2

Pleat

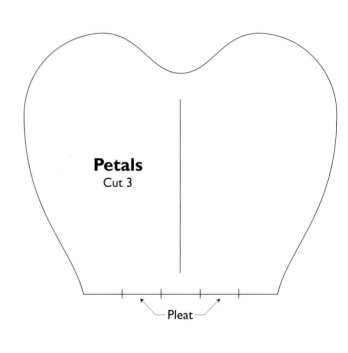

Petals
Cut 3

Pleat

The knitted flowers on the dining room chairs are a fun
and whimsical play on the rug design.

Design by Alma Allen • Sewing by Alma Allen • Quilting by Jeanne Zyck

Chocolate Blooms

PROJECT SIZE: 62" x 72"

INSTRUCTIONS

Cutting measurements include a 1/4" seam allowance.

APPLIQUÉ BLOCKS

❖ Cut 7 – 8" squares from a light floral print. Cut 5 – 8" squares from a different light print. Set 5 squares aside.

❖ Make templates of the appliqué shapes. Refer to the template page and cut out the pieces needed for each block.

❖ Use the Clover bias tape maker and make 42" of 3/8" bias tape from a green & chocolate check for stems. Make 7 stems 6" long.

❖ Refer to the placement diagram and position the pieces on the background block.

❖ Baste the pieces on the block and appliqué them in place.

Supply List

❖ 3 1/4 yds. of a light floral print for the borders, side triangles, corner triangles, alternating blocks and pieced blocks
❖ 1 1/4 yd. of a different light floral print for side triangles, alternating blocks and pieced blocks
❖ 1/4 yd. each of 5 red prints for the pieced blocks and flower centers
❖ 1/2 yd. of a large scale red print for the border and blocks
❖ 1/6 yd. each of 3 chocolate prints for the blocks and flowers
❖ Fat quarter of green & chocolate check for the flower stems
❖ Fat quarter each of 3 different green prints for the leaves
❖ 3/8" Clover bias tape maker

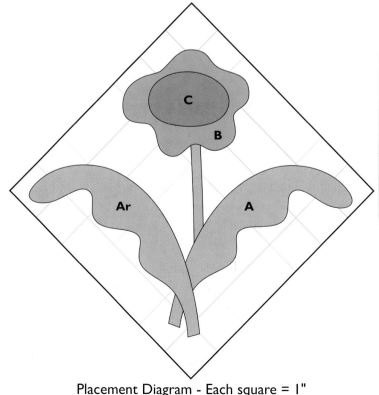

Placement Diagram - Each square = 1"

❖ Repeat for 7 appliqué blocks. Set the blocks aside.

PIECED BLOCKS

❖ Cut 250 – 2" squares from an assortment of red prints.

❖ Cut 320 – 2" squares from an assortment of light prints.

❖ Cut 90 – 2" squares from an assortment of chocolate prints.

❖ Refer to the diagram and sew 20 - 9-patch blocks. Note 9 of the blocks have one or two chocolate squares replacing the red squares.

❖ Place one light square and one red square right sides together. Sew a seam along the diagonal as illustrated in Diagram A.

❖ Trim away the excess fabric as illustrated in Diagram B.

Diagram A   Diagram B   Diagram C

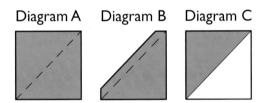

❖ Open the half-square triangle units as illustrated in Diagram C and press. Repeat for 160 units.

❖ Refer to the diagram and sew the 20 blocks together.

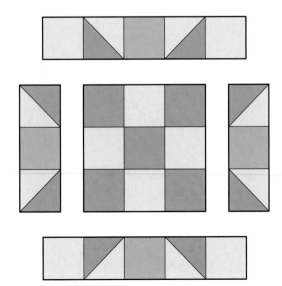

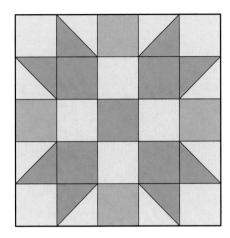

SIDE TRIANGLES, CORNER TRIANGLES & BORDERS

❖ Cut 2 – 11 7/8" squares from a light print. Cut 2 – 11 7/8" squares from a different light print. Cut each square in half twice on the diagonal. These will be the side triangles. There will be two extra triangles.

❖ Cut 2 – 6 1/4" squares from a light print. Cut each in half once on the diagonal. These will be the corner triangles.

❖ Refer to the picture and sew the quilt top together.

❖ Cut 5 strips 2" wide from a red floral print. Sew them together in a continuous strip. From this length cut 2 strips 2" x 53 5/8". Sew one strip to each side of the quilt top.

❖ Cut 2 strips from the remaining length, 2" x 46". Sew one strip each to the top and bottom of the quilt top.

❖ Cut 2 strips 8 1/2" x 56 5/8" from a light floral print. Sew one strip to each side of the quilt top.

❖ Cut 2 strips 8 1/2" x 62" from a light floral print. Sew one strip each to the top and bottom of the quilt top.

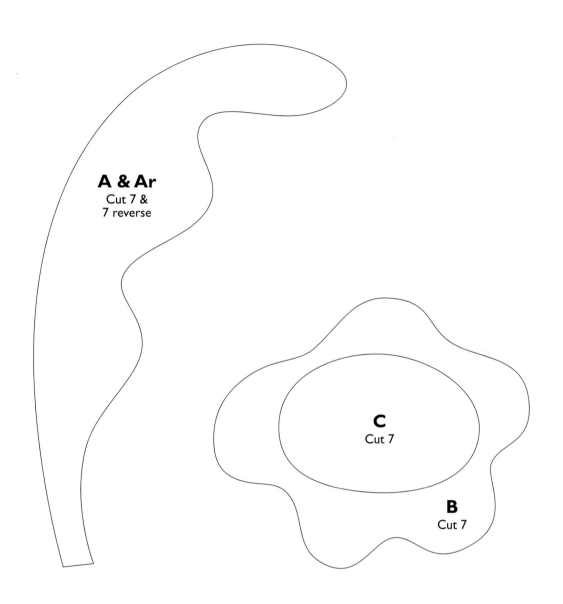

A & Ar
Cut 7 &
7 reverse

C
Cut 7

B
Cut 7

Design by Alma Allen • Sewing by Alma Allen

Floral Pincushion

PROJECT SIZE: 3½" x 4½"

INSTRUCTIONS

Cutting measurements include a 1/4" seam allowance.

❖ Cut the background 4" x 5" from dark wool. Cut the pincushion backing 4" x 5" from the green prairie cloth.

❖ Make templates of the appliqué shapes. Refer to the templates and cut out the pieces needed.

❖ Cut a 5 1/2" x 1/4" strip from the light tan wool for the stem.

❖ Refer to the picture and position the pieces on the background block.

❖ Refer to the directions on the Clover yo-yo maker and make one large flower.

❖ Baste the pieces on the block and appliqué them in place.

❖ Sew the pincushion front to the back right sides together. Use a 1/4" seam allowance. Leave a 3" opening on the bottom seam for turning.

❖ Turn and stuff with poly-fil. Blind stitch the opening closed.

Supply List

❖ Scrap of dark wool for background
❖ Scrap of green prairie cloth for backing
❖ Scrap of light tan wool for stem
❖ Scrap of brown check wool for leaves
❖ Scrap of green print for leaves
❖ Scrap of red print for flower
❖ Clover yo-yo maker – flower shaped, large
❖ Poly-fil

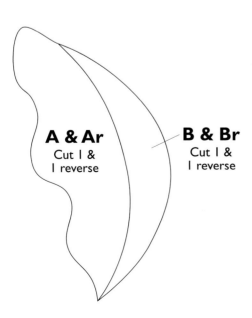

A & Ar
Cut 1 &
1 reverse

B & Br
Cut 1 &
1 reverse

Design by Barb Adams • Sewing by Leona Adams • Quilting by Jeanne Zyck

Rick Rack Garden

PROJECT SIZE: 80" x 80"

INSTRUCTIONS

Cutting measurements include a 1/4" seam allowance.

PIECED VARIABLE STAR BLOCK

❖ Refer to the block diagram on page 82 and cut 1 – 9 1/2" square from a light print for the center.

❖ Cut 4 – 5" squares from a light print for the corners.

❖ Cut 1 – 10 1/4" square from a light print for the "flying geese" units. Cut on the diagonal twice.

❖ Cut 4 – 5 3/8" squares from a dark print for the flying geese units. Cut each square once diagonally.

❖ Piece 4 flying geese units.

❖ Sew the block together and repeat for 9 variable star blocks.

RICK RACK

❖ Refer to the instructions for dyeing the rick rack on page 80. Dye all 10 yards of the large rick rack green. Dye 8 yards of the small rick rack green. Dye 1 yard of the small rick rack brown.

APPLIQUÉ BLOCK I

❖ Choose one of the completed pieced variable star blocks. This block will serve as the background for the appliqué. Refer to the placement diagram on page 84 and note the templates needed for this block. Refer to the template page and make the templates of the appliqué shapes. Cut out the pieces needed for the block.

❖ Refer to the placement diagram and position the pieces on the background block. Use the small green rick rack for the stems.

❖ Baste the pieces on the block and appliqué them in place.

❖ Set the appliqué block aside.

DYEING THE RICK RACK

Results may vary with any dyeing procedure. To dye rick rack follow the directions on back of the dye package. An additional yard of rick rack is provided in the fabric requirements to allow for experimentation.

Green dye mix for 8 yds. small rick rack and 10 yds. of large rick rack:
- 2 quarts of warm water
- 2 T of #56 Green
- 2 2/3 tsp. of #05 Sunflower
- 2/3 tsp. of #55 Burnt Orange
- 8 tablespoons of salt

Brown dye mix for 1 yd. of small rick rack:
For the brown color mix:
- 2 cups of warm water
- 1 T. of #11 Dark Brown
- 2 tablespoons of salt

- Cut 6" from dampened rick rack and place in dye. Stir for 15 minutes.

- Remove the piece of rick rack and rinse well under running water.

- Once the color looks correct, dampen the rick rack and place all of the rick rack into the dye pot. To make the trim colorfast, follow the package instructions closely after the rick rack has been dyed.

- Blot rick rack with a towel. Spread the dyed rick rack out on a flat surface and allow to air dry.

APPLIQUÉ BLOCK 2

- Again, choose one of the completed pieced variable star blocks. This block will serve as the background for the appliqué. Refer to the placement diagram on page 86 and note the templates needed for this block. Refer to the template page and make the templates of the appliqué shapes. Cut out the pieces needed for the block.

- Refer to the placement diagram and position the pieces on the background block. Use the small green rick rack for the stems.

- Baste the pieces on the block and appliqué them in place.

- Set the appliqué block aside.

APPLIQUÉ BLOCK 3

- Again, choose one of the completed pieced variable star blocks. This block will serve as the background for the appliqué. Refer to the placement diagram on page 88 and note the templates needed for this block. Refer to the template page and make the templates of the appliqué shapes. Cut out the pieces needed for the block.

- Refer to the placement diagram and position the pieces on the background block. Use the small brown rick rack for the stems.

- Baste the pieces on the block and appliqué them in place.

- Set the appliqué block aside.

APPLIQUÉ BLOCK 4

- Again, choose one of the completed pieced variable star blocks. This block will serve as the background for the appliqué. Refer to the placement diagram on page 90 and note the templates needed for this block. Refer to the template page and make the templates of the appliqué shapes. Cut out the pieces needed for the block.

- Refer to the placement diagram and position the pieces on the background block. Use the small green rick rack for the stems.

- Baste the pieces on the block and appliqué them in place.

- Set the appliqué block aside.

APPLIQUÉ BLOCK 5

- Again, choose one of the completed pieced variable star blocks. This block will serve as the background for the appliqué. Refer to the placement diagram on page 92 and note the templates needed for this block. Refer to the template page and make the templates of the appliqué shapes. Cut out the pieces needed for the block.

- Refer to the placement diagram and position the pieces on the background block. Use the small green rick rack for the stems.

❖ Baste the pieces on the block and appliqué them in place.

❖ Set the appliqué block aside.

❖ Repeat for 5 blocks.

SASHING

❖ Cut 6 – 3 1/2" x 18 1/2" strips for vertical sashing.

❖ Piece together 3 1/2" strips to make 2 – 3 1/2" x 60 1/2" strips for horizontal sashing.

❖ Refer to the quilt layout diagram on page 83 and sew the blocks and sashing together.

PIECED BORDER

❖ Use your favorite method and make 120 – 2" finished half-square triangles from the light fern print and the large-scale green print.

❖ Refer to the Quilt Layout Diagram on page 83 and sew 2 strips of 30 half-square triangle units each. Sew one strip to each side of the quilt top.

❖ Cut 4 – 2 1/2" squares from the large-scale green print. These will be the corner squares.

❖ Sew 2 strips of 30 units each. Begin and end each strip with one green square. Sew one strip to the top and one to the bottom of the quilt top.

FABRIC BORDER

❖ Cut 2 border strips 8 1/2" x 64 1/2" from the large-scale green print. Sew one strip to each side of the quilt top.
❖ Cut 2 border strips 8 1/2" x 80 1/2" from the large-scale green print. Sew one strip to the top and one to the bottom of the quilt top.

RICK RACK BINDING

❖ Cut 9 yds. of 2" bias strips from the backing fabric for the binding.

❖ Quilt the quilt before adding the rick rack binding. Pin the rick rack along the right side of the quilt top continuing around each edge. Add a bit of extra rick rack as you pin around each corner. Clip if needed. When you stitch around the entire quilt and get to the place where you started, fold the raw rick rack edge over into the seam allowance and overlap the rick rack a bit. Machine baste into place.

❖ Sew the binding on, sandwiching the rick rack between the quilt top and binding. Turn the binding towards the back, turn under your seam allowance and whip-stitch in place.

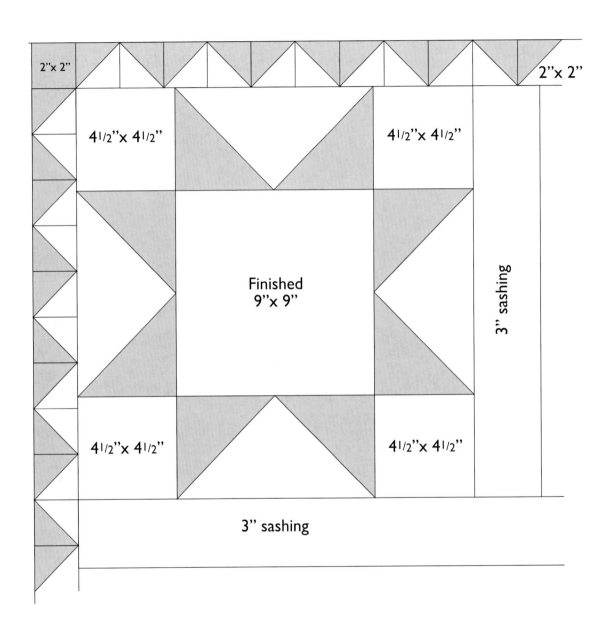

2"x 2"

2"x 2"

4¹/2"x 4¹/2"

4¹/2"x 4¹/2"

Finished
9"x 9"

3" sashing

4¹/2"x 4¹/2"

4¹/2"x 4¹/2"

3" sashing

Block Diagram

Total 80" x 80"

Border – 8" wide

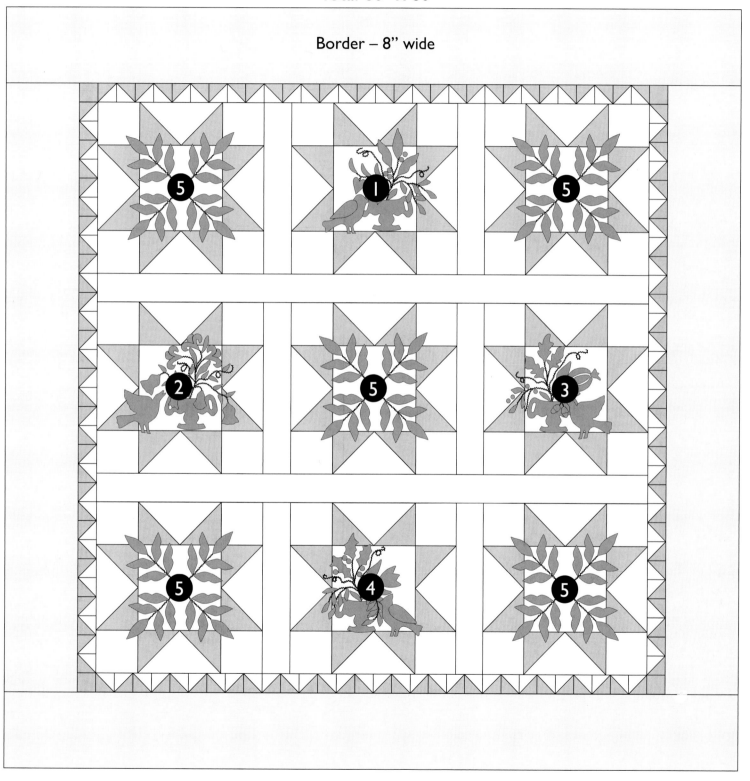

Quilt Layout Diagram

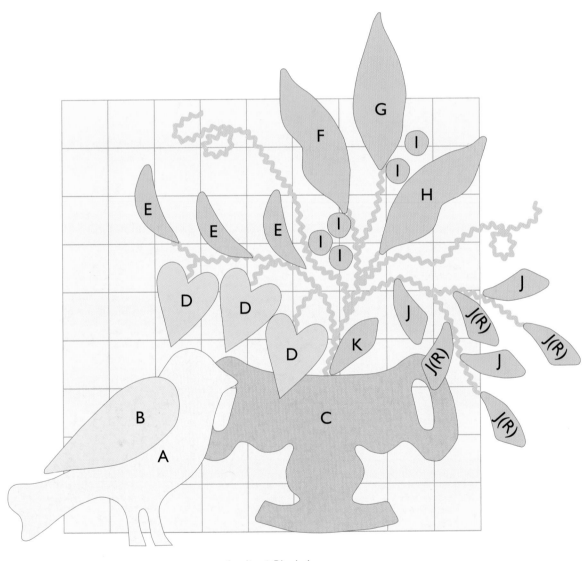

Appliqué Block 1
Placement Diagram

I
Cut 5

Cut 3 and
4 reversed

J

K

H

G

F

E
Cut 3

B

A

D
Cut 3

C

Appliqué Block 1
Templates

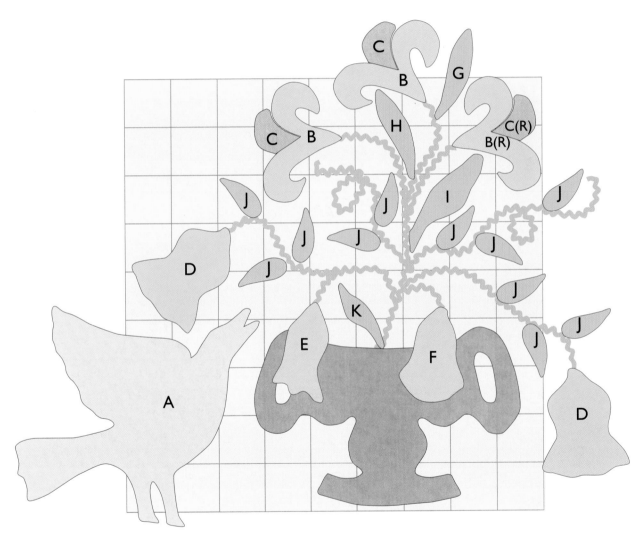

Appliqué Block 2
Placement Diagram

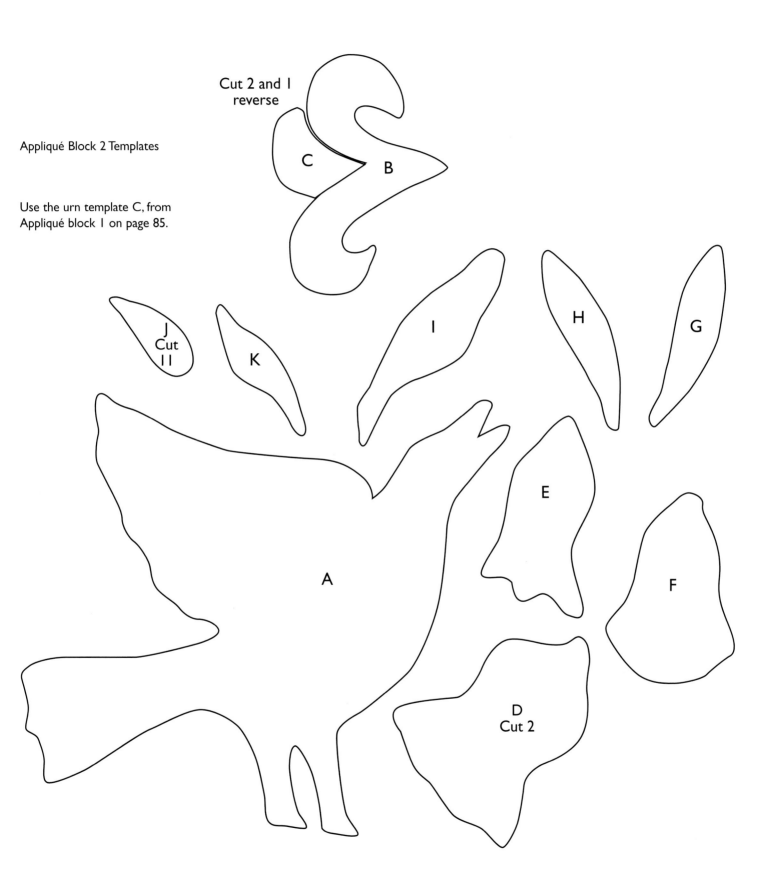

Cut 2 and 1
reverse

Appliqué Block 2 Templates

Use the urn template C, from
Appliqué block 1 on page 85.

C

B

J
Cut
11

K

I

H

G

A

E

F

D
Cut 2

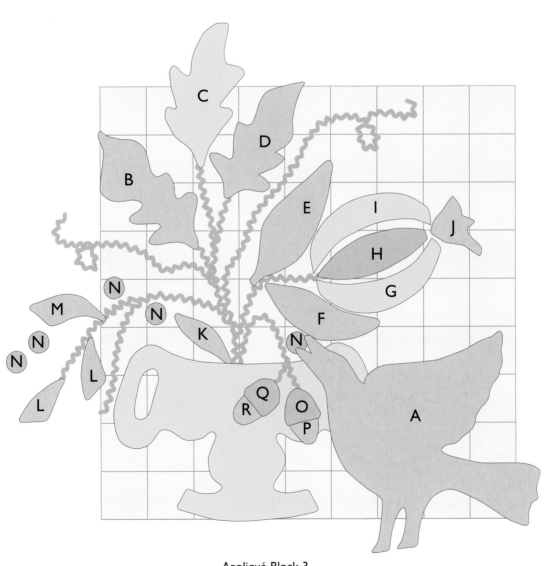

Appliqué Block 3
Placement Diagram

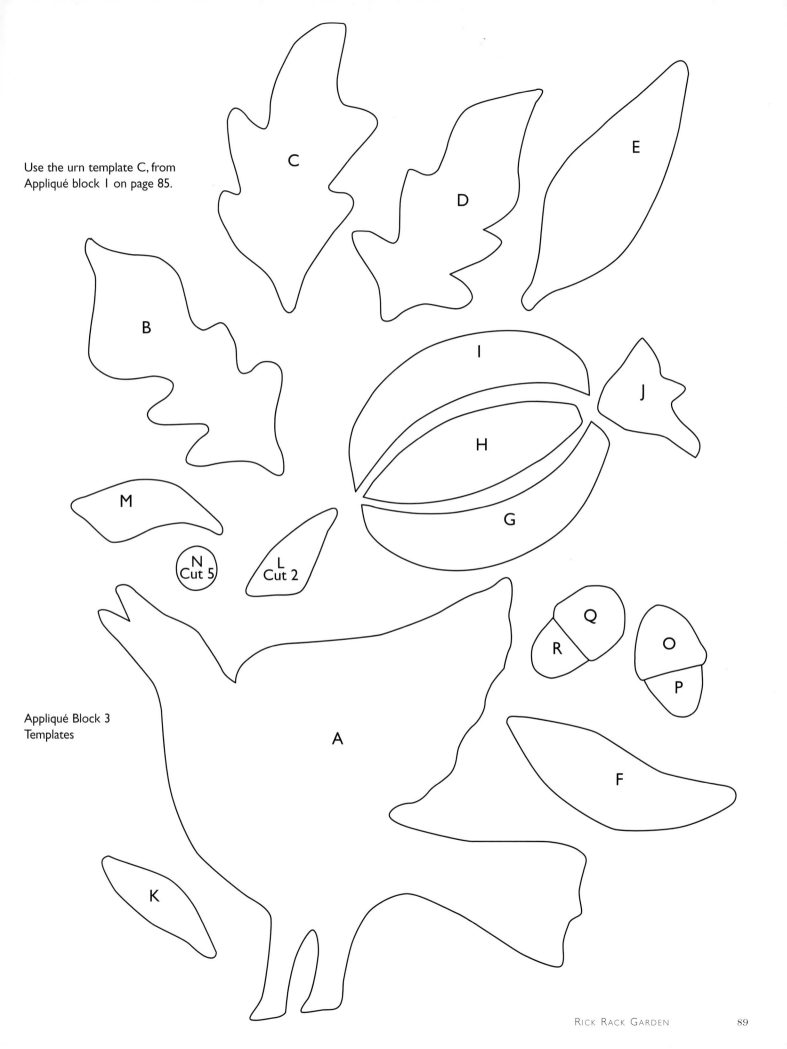

Use the urn template C, from
Appliqué block 1 on page 85.

C

D

E

B

I

J

H

G

M

N
Cut 5

L
Cut 2

Q

R

O

P

A

Appliqué Block 3
Templates

F

K

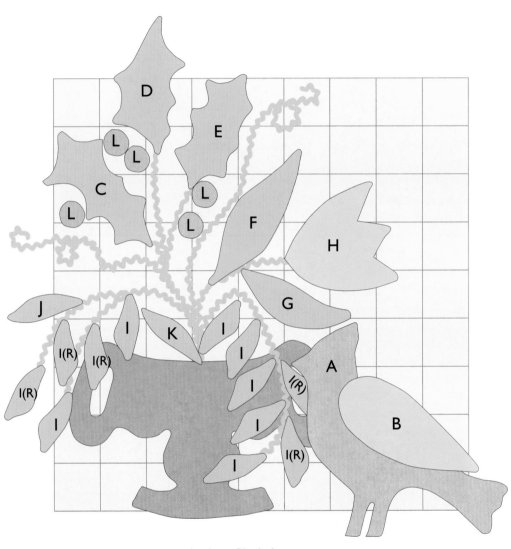

Appliqué Block 4
Placement Diagram

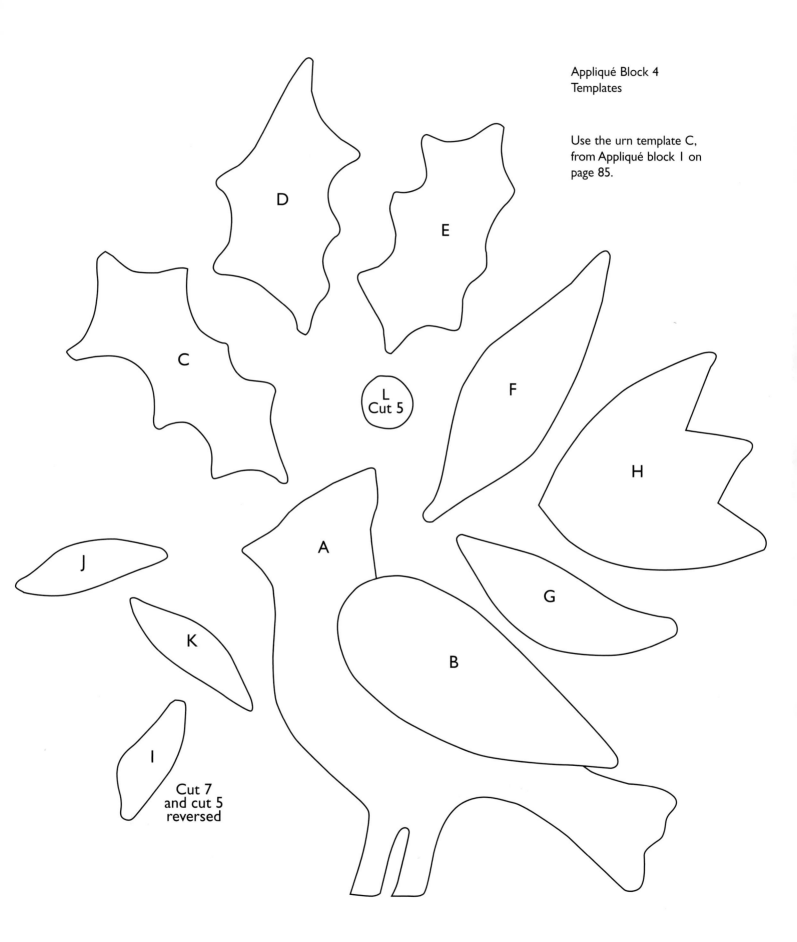

Appliqué Block 4
Templates

Use the urn template C,
from Appliqué block 1 on
page 85.

D

E

C

L
Cut 5

F

H

A

G

J

K

B

I

Cut 7
and cut 5
reversed

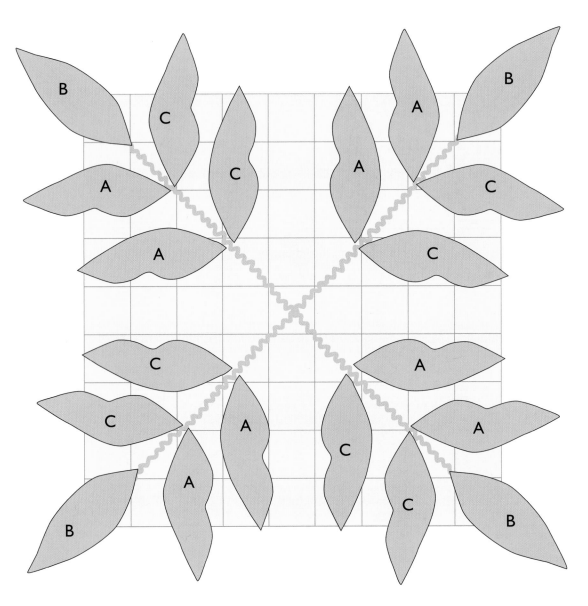

Appliqué Block 5
Placement Diagram

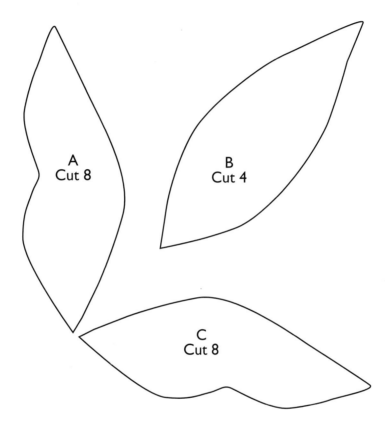

A
Cut 8

B
Cut 4

C
Cut 8

Appliqué Block 5
Templates

Other Star Books

- *One Piece at a Time* by Kansas City Star Books – 1999

- *More Kansas City Star Quilts* by Kansas City Star Books – 2000

- *Outside the Box: Hexagon Patterns from The Kansas City Star* by Edie McGinnis – 2001

- *Prairie Flower: A Year on the Plains* by Barbara Brackman – 2001

- *The Sister Blocks* by Edie McGinnis – 2001

- *Kansas City Quilt Makers* by Doug Worgul – 2001

- *O' Glory: Americana Quilts Blocks from The Kansas City Star* by Edie McGinnis – 2001

- *Hearts & Flowers: Hand Applique from Start to Finish* by Kathy Delaney – 2002

- *Roads & Curves Ahead* by Edie McGinnis – 2002

- ***Celebration of American Life: Applique Patterns Honoring a Nation and Its People* by Barb Adams and Alma Allen – 2002**

- ***Women of Grace & Charm: A Quilting Tribute to the Women Who Served in World War II* by Barb Adams and Alma Allen – 2003**

- *A Heartland Album: More Techniques in Hand Appliqué* by Kathy Delaney – 2003

- *Quilting a Poem: Designs Inspired by America's Poets* by Frances Kite and Debra Rowden – 2003

- *Carolyn's Paper Pieced Garden: Patterns for Miniature and Full-Sized Quilts* by Carolyn Cullinan McCormick – 2003

- *Friendships in Bloom: Round Robin Quilts* by Marjorie Nelson and Rebecca Nelson-Zerfas – 2003

- *Baskets of Treasures: Designs Inspired by Life Along the River* by Edie McGinnis – 2003

- *Heart & Home: Unique American Women and the Houses that Inspire* by Kathy Schmitz – 2003

- *Women of Design: Quilts in the Newspaper* by Barbara Brackman – 2004

- *The Basics: An Easy Guide to Beginning Quiltmaking* by Kathy Delaney – 2004

- *Four Block Quilts: Echoes of History, Pieced Boldly & Appliqued Freely* by Terry Clothier Thompson – 2004

- *No Boundaries: Bringing Your Fabric Over the Edge* by Edie McGinnis – 2004

- *Horn of Plenty for a New Century* by Kathy Delaney – 2004

- ***Quilting the Garden* by Barb Adams and Alma Allen – 2004**

- *Stars All Around Us: Quilts and Projects Inspired by a Beloved Symbol* by Cherie Ralston – 2005

- *Quilters' Stories: Collecting History in the Heart of America* by Debra Rowden – 2005

- *Libertyville: Where Liberty Dwells, There is My Country* by Terry Clothier Thompson – 2005

- *Sparkling Jewels, Pearls of Wisdom* by Edie McGinnis – 2005

- *Grapefruit Juice & Sugar* by Jenifer Dick – 2005

- ***Home Sweet Home* by Barb Adams and Alma Allen – 2005**

- *Patterns of History: The Challenge Winners* by Kathy Delaney – 2005

- *My Quilt Stories* by Debra Rowden – 2005

- *Quilts in Red and Green and the Women Who Made Them* by Nancy Hornback and Terry Clothier Thompson – 2006

- *Hard Times, Splendid Quilts: A 1930s Celebration, Paper Piecing from The Kansas City Star* by Carolyn Cullinan McCormick – 2006

- *Art Nouveau Quilts for the 21st Century* by Bea Oglesby – 2006

- *Designer Quilts: Great Projects from Moda's Best Fabric Artists* – 2006

- *Birds of a Feather* **by Barb Adams and Alma Allen – 2006**

- *Feedsacks! Beautiful Quilts from Humble Beginnings* by Edie McGinnis – 2006

- *Kansas Spirit: Historical Quilt Blocks and the Saga of the Sunflower State* by Jeanne Poore – 2006

- *Bold Improvisation: Searching for African American Quilts – The Heffley Collection* by Scott Heffley – 2007

- *The Soulful Art of African American Quilts: Nineteen Bold, Improvisational Projects* by Sonie Ruffin – 2007

- *Alphabet Quilts: Letters for All Ages* by Bea Oglesby –2007

- *Beyond the Basics: A Potpourri of Quiltmaking Techniques* by Kathy Delaney – Fall – 2007

- *Golden's Journal: 20 Sampler Blocks Honoring Prairie Farm Life* by Christina DeArmond, Eula Lang and Kaye Spitzli – Fall – 2007

- *Borderland in Butternut and Blue: A Sampler Quilt to Recall the Civil War Along the Kansas/Missouri Border* by Barbara Brackman – Fall – 2007

- *Come to the Fair! Quilts that Celebrate State Fair Traditions* by Edie McGinnis – Fall – 2007

- *Cotton and Wool: Miss Jump's Farewell* by Linda Brannock – Fall – 2007

QUEEN BEES MYSTERIES:

- *Murders on Elderberry Road* by Sally Goldenbaum – 2003

- *A Murder of Taste* by Sally Goldenbaum – 2004

- *Murder on a Starry Night* by Sally Goldenbaum – 2005

PROJECT BOOKS:

- *Fan Quilt Memories* by Jeanne Poore – 2000

- *Santa's Parade of Nursery Rhymes* by Jeanne Poore – 2001

- *As the Crow Flies* by Edie McGinnis – 2007

- *Sweet Inspirations* by Pam Manning – 2007

- *Quilts Through the Camera's Eye* by Terry Clothier Thompson – Fall – 2007